# AN EVENT-BASED SCIENCE MODULE

# ASTEROID!

## STUDENT EDITION

## Russell G. Wright

PEARSON

Prentice Hall

Boston, Massachusetts
Upper Saddle River, New Jersey

The developers of Event-Based Science (EBS) have been encouraged and supported at every step in the creative process by the Superintendent and Board of Education of Montgomery County Public Schools, Rockville, Maryland (MCPS). The superintendent and board are committed to the systemic improvement of science instruction, grades preK–12. EBS is one of many projects undertaken to ensure the scientific literacy of all students.

The developers of *Asteroid!* pay special tribute to the editors, publisher, and reporters of *USA TODAY*. Without their cooperation and support, the creation of this module would not have been possible.

Photographs: Cover Tom Bean, Tony Stone Images; pages 3, 4, 6, 11, 20–22, 27, 28, 31–39, 41, 45, and 47–49 National Aeronautics and Space Administration; page 12 R. E. Schmidt of the U. S. Naval Observatory; page 13 U. S. Naval Observatory; page 18 National Oceanic and Atmospheric Administration; page 28 Matt Mendelsohn, *USA TODAY;* all "Student Voices" Frank Weisel and Gene Molesky.

This material is based upon work supported by the National Science Foundation under grant number MDR-9154094. Any opinions, findings, conclusions, or recommendations expressed in this publication are those of the Event-Based Science Project and do not necessarily reflect the views of the National Science Foundation.

ISBN: 0-13-166633-9

3 4 5 6 7 8 9 10    10 09 08 07 06

# Contents

# Project Team

## Author

Russell G. Wright, with contributions from Leonard David, Barbara Sprungman, and the following teachers:

*Nancy A. Carey, Col. E. Brooke Lee Middle School, Silver Spring, Maryland

*Charles E. Doebler, Robert Frost Middle School, Rockville, Maryland

*Bernard J. Hudock, Watkins Mill High School, Gaithersburg, Maryland

*Nell Jeter, Earle B. Wood Middle School, Rockville, Maryland

*Cynthia Johnson-Cash, Ridgeview Middle School, Gaithersburg, Maryland

*Jeanne S. Klugel, Col. E. Brooke Lee Middle School, Silver Spring, Maryland

*Harry P. Mazur, Parkland Middle School, Rockville, Maryland

*Eugene M. Molesky, Ridgeview Middle School, Gaithersburg, Maryland

*Joseph M. Panarella, Montgomery Village Middle School, Gaithersburg, Maryland

*John Senuta, Ridgeview Middle School, Gaithersburg, Maryland

*J. Martin Smiley, Gaithersburg Middle School, Gaithersburg, Maryland

*Thomas G. Smith, Briggs Chaney Middle School, Silver Spring, Maryland

*Frank S. Weisel, Poolesville Junior/Senior High School, Poolesville, Maryland

Evan D. Wolff (teacher in training), University of Maryland, College Park, Maryland

## Event/Site Support

Gene Molesky, Gaithersburg, Maryland

Frank Weisel, Poolesville, Maryland

Katie Baird, Prescott, Arizona

## Scientific Reviewers

Andrew Fraknoi, Astronomical Society of the Pacific

Clark R. Chapman, Planetary Science Institute

Dorothy K. Hall, L. Walter, Dave Stevens, Charles Boyle, and Nahid Khazenie, National Aeronautics and Space Administration

Ramon E. Lopez, University of Maryland

## Student Consultants

*Redland Middle School, Rockville, Maryland: Nina Armah, Laura-Marie Armstrong, Erick Carlson, Luis Castro, Alison Dean, Laura Downing, Monique Frazier, Paul Hayes, Jr., Brian Houska, Lise Hyon, Halima Karzai, Erin Kerman, Anne Kiang, Ethan Lee, Gloria Lee, Genevieve Maricle, Rebecca Marshall, Lawrence Matthews, Jr., Melissa Mong, Roxanna Nwachukwu, Jereme Price, Becky Richardson, Gina Romano, Crystal Shirley, Nathan Unce, Daniel Weimer, Sommer Yirka

*Ridgeview Intermediate School, Gaithersburg, Maryland: Sean Shillinger

## EBS Advisory Committee

Dr. Eddie Anderson, National Aeronautics and Space Administration

Ms. Mary Ann Brearton, American Association for the Advancement of Science

Dr. Lynn Dierking, National Museum of American History

Mr. Bob Dubill, *USA Today*

Mr. Herbert Freiberger, United States Geological Survey

Ms. Joyce Gross, National Oceanic and Atmospheric Administration

Dr. Harry Herzer, National Aeronautic and Space Administration

Mr. Frank Ireton, American Geophysical Union

*Mr. Bill Krayer, Gaithersburg High School

Dr. Ivo Lindauer, National Science Foundation

Dr. Rocky Lopes, American Red Cross

*Dr. Jerry Lynch, John T. Baker Middle School,

Ms. Virginia Major, United States Geological Survey

Ms. Marilyn P. McCabe, Federal Emergency Management Agency

Mr. John Ortman, United States Department of Energy

Dr. Noel Raufaste, Jr., National Institute of Standards and Technology

Dr. Bill Sacco, Trianalytics Corporation

Mr. Ron Slotkin, United States Environmental Protection Agency

Ms. Katarina Stenstedt, Addison-Wesley Publishing Co.

*Montgomery County Public Schools

# Preface

## The Event-Based Science Model

*Asteroid!* is a student module about astronomy that follows the Event-Based Science (EBS) Instructional Model. You will watch "live" CNN news coverage about objects from space that have hit or just missed hitting Earth, and read *USA Today* reports about these types of events. Your discussions about these impact events will show you and your teacher that you already know a lot about the astronomy concepts in these events. Next, a real-world task puts you and your classmates in the roles of people who must use scientific knowledge and processes to solve a problem related to out-of-this-world impacts. You will probably need more information before you start the task. If you do, *Asteroid!* provides hands-on activities and a variety of reading materials to give you some of the background you need. About halfway through the module, you will be ready to begin the task. Your teacher will assign you a role to play and turn you and your team loose to complete the task. You will spend the rest of the time in this unit working on that task.

## Scientific Literacy

Today, a literate citizen is expected to know more than how to read, write, and do simple arithmetic. Today, literacy includes knowing how to analyze problems, ask critical questions, and explain events. A literate citizen must also be able to apply scientific knowledge and processes to new situations. Event-Based Science allows you to practice these skills by placing the study of science in a meaningful context.

Knowledge cannot be transferred to your mind from the mind of your teacher, or from the pages of a textbook. Nor can knowledge occur in isolation from the other things you know about and have experienced in the real world. The Event-Based Science model is based on the idea that the best way to know something is to be actively engaged in it.

Therefore, the Event-Based Science model simulates real-life events and experiences to make your learning more authentic and memorable. First, the event is brought to life through television news coverage. Viewing the news allows you to be there "as it happened," and that is as close as you can get to actually experiencing the event. Second, by simulating the kinds of teamwork and problem solving that occur every day in our workplaces and communities, you will experience the role that scientific knowledge and teamwork play in the lives of ordinary people. Thus *Asteroid!* is built around simulations of real-life events and experiences that affected people's lives and environments dramatically.

In an Event-Based Science classroom, you become the workers, your product is a solution to a real problem, and your teacher is your coach, guide, and advisor. You will be assessed on how you use scientific processes and concepts to solve problems as well as on the quality of your work.

One of the primary goals of the EBS Project is to place the learning of science in a real-world context and to make scientific learning fun. You should not allow yourself to become frustrated. If you cannot find a specific piece of information, it's okay to be creative.

## Student Resources

*Asteroid!* is unlike a regular textbook. An Event-Based Science module tells a story about a real event; it has real newspaper articles about the event, and inserts that explain the scientific concepts involved in the event. It also contains laboratory investigations for you to conduct in your science class, and activities that you may do in

English, math, social studies, or technology education classes. In addition, an Event-Based Science module gives you and your classmates a real-world task to do. The task is always done by teams of students, with each team member performing a real-life role, while completing an important part of the task. The task cannot be completed without you and everyone else on your team doing their parts. The team approach allows you to share your knowledge and strengths. It also helps you learn to work with a team in a real-world situation. Today, most professionals work in teams.

Interviews with people who actually serve in the roles you are playing are scattered throughout the Event-Based Science module. Middle school students who actually experienced the event tell their stories throughout the module too.

Since this module is unlike a regular textbook, you have much more flexibility in using it.

- You may read **The Story** for enjoyment or to find clues that will help you tackle your part of the task.
- You may read selections from the **Discovery File** when you need help understanding something in the story or when you need help with the task.
- You may read all the **On the Job** features because you are curious about what professionals do, or you may read only the interview with the professional who works in the role you've chosen because it may give you ideas that will help you complete the task.
- You may read the **In the News** features because they catch your eye, or as part of your search for information.
- You will probably read all the **Student Voices** features because they are interesting stories told by middle school students like yourself.

*Asteroid!* is also unlike regular textbooks in that the collection of resources found in it is not meant to be complete. You must find additional information from other sources, too. Textbooks, encyclopedias, pamphlets, magazine and newspaper articles, videos, films, filmstrips, the Internet, and people in your community are all potential sources of useful information. If you have access to the World Wide Web, you will want to visit the Event-Based Science home page (www.PHSchool.com/EBS), where you will find links to other sites around the world with information and people that will be very helpful to you. It is vital to your preparation as a scientifically literate citizen of the twenty-first century that you get used to finding information on your own.

The shape of a new form of science education is beginning to emerge, and the Event-Based Science Project is leading the way. We hope you enjoy your experience with this module as much as we enjoyed developing it.

—Russell G. Wright, Ed.D.
Project Director and Principal Author

# Out of Time

It tumbled through the vast darkness of space—a rocky mini-world billions of years old. As if in a game of cosmic pool, the massive hulk careened toward the Sun's third planet: Earth. It sliced through Earth's layers of atmosphere, becoming ever brighter and radiating a glow greater than that of the Sun.

As it slammed into the ground, it released millions of megatons of explosive energy. It scarred the terrain with a 100-mile-wide crater. The blast that rumbled outward from the hit sparked massive forest fires and hurled billions of tons of rock and debris in every direction. Pulverized material from the impact were tossed miles high into the atmosphere.

The dust and debris drifted around Earth, carried by upper atmospheric winds. A mix of acid rain and a nitric-oxide smog spread across the planet. Sunlight disappeared as if an immense window shade had been drawn. Earth was in darkness for months, then years. Each day, high noon was nothing more than a dusty pale sky.

Slowly, the lack of sunlight cooled Earth. Photosynthesis in the plants and trees became crippled while the cloak of darkness engulfed the planet. In the oceans, photosynthesizing plankton began to die. This disrupted the marine food chain so much that it collapsed. Much of the life on Earth struggled to stay alive, faltered, then died away.

The thought of a gigantic rock hitting Earth and throwing life into peril might seem unreal. However, it may have happened in Earth's prehistory. And it could happen any time in the future. It could even happen within the few seconds it takes you to read this sentence.

Astronomers believe there are thousands of asteroids moving through space. Asteroids are small worlds of aggregated minerals and metals without atmospheres. A great number of asteroids are on paths that cross the orbit of Earth, making our planet in a very real sense a moving target.

Comets, on the other hand, consist of rock and dust mixed with frozen ice and gases. The frozen materials stream off into space to form tails as the comets are warmed by the Sun during their treks through the solar system. It is thought that a comet, when depleted of its icy mass, is left looking like an asteroid.

When I was a little kid, about four, my dad and I were sitting outside. We were watching the sky. My dad told me about a meteor shower that was coming. So we waited. I didn't know what a meteor shower was. I was really into it. About 8:00 P.M., we saw a little one pass by. I saw it, but not very well. Five minutes later we saw about 20 of them shoot by. It was so cool. I had never seen anything like it. I was so amazed that I wanted to stay out there the entire night, but it stopped, and I went back inside.

RAY TANG
PRESCOTT, ARIZONA

You could call asteroids solar system leftovers. The origins of asteroids are believed to be linked to the natural outcome of planetary formation early in the solar system. If so, asteroids are time capsules—specimens of ancient matter awaiting scientific scrutiny.

For the most part, asteroids are huddled in a zone between the orbits of Mars and Jupiter. As many as 30,000 of these chunks of rock are estimated to reside in what is called the *asteroid belt*. For many years, scientists theorized that this main belt of asteroids, if clumped together, represented a missing planet that lost in a gravitational tug of war. But scientists no longer believe this to be the case. Debate still rages as to exactly how the asteroids were formed.

The main cluster of asteroids between Mars and Jupiter is about 2.8 astronomical units (AU) from the Sun. One AU equals the mean distance of Earth from the Sun or 149.6 million kilometers.

Some asteroids' orbits take them into the inner regions of the solar system. They are called Earth-approaching asteroids. These rocky hulks are fragments of main belt asteroids. Some are burned-out comets. Earth-approaching asteroids fall into two classes: *Amor* asteroids have orbits beyond Earth's orbit, but at some point cross inside the orbit of Mars, and *Apollo* asteroids pass inside Earth's orbit. ■

**IN THE NEWS**

# Comets may have caused extinctions

Asteroids and comets that crashed to Earth millions of years ago may have started the breakup of an ancient supercontinent known as Gondwanaland, NASA scientists said Tuesday. The three scientists from NASA's Ames Research Center near San Francisco, said asteroids and comets — not glaciers — also may have led to mass extinctions of animals. Scientist Verne Oberbeck said the finding could "radically" change current views. The theory will be detailed this week at a San Francisco meeting of the American Geophysical Union.

**IN THE NEWS**

# Ancient asteroid crater a billion-year rarity

By Tim Friend
USA TODAY

An asteroid collision linked to the end of the dinosaur era may have packed the biggest punch in the solar system in the past several billion years.

The report in today's *Science* adds fuel to the debate on dinosaur extinction — whether they were wiped out by the effects of an asteroid smashing into the Earth or died off more slowly due to climate and geological changes.

Research suggests the Chicxulub crater in northern Yucatan, Mexico, is nearly twice as big as thought: 190 miles across vs. 112 miles (the map shows how large the crater would be if it were on the East Coast).

That boosts the possibility the impact caused a mass extinction 65 million years ago, says Virgil Sharpton of Houston's Lunar and Planetary Institute.

The crater size also suggests such a collision is much rarer, occurring only once every 1 billion or 2 billion years.

The larger size was determined by measuring differences in the pull of gravity from the crater center to its edge, like rings of water in a pool.

Says Sharpton: The pattern is like "the largest impact craters ... on any planet so its potential for initiating global catastrophe goes up considerably."

Scientists point to a layer of clay deposited 65 million years ago as evidence the collision threw up a global dust cloud that blocked the sun and eventually killed the dinosaurs.

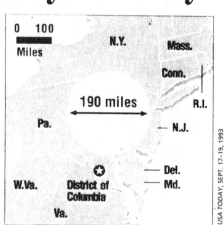

By Stephen Conley, USA TODAY

USA TODAY, SEPT. 17–19, 1993

# What Is an Asteroid?

About 6,000 asteroids had been catalogued by 1993. Astronomers estimate there could be as many as a billion asteroids and comets yet undiscovered. Maybe you will be among the future astronomers who discover some of these celestial bodies.

Many asteroids and comets have remained unchanged since the formative stages of our solar system, and they are thought to hold answers to some of the unsolved mysteries about the solar system's origins.

Asteroids range in size from the largest known, Ceres, which measures 940 kilometers (584 miles) across, to some smaller than the size of a football field. Few are larger than 300 kilometers (186 miles).

Telescope observations as well as close-up looks by spacecraft show that there are distinct classes of asteroids. Their color and composition differ, not only from planets and their moons, but also among themselves.

Some asteroids contain small quantities of water locked up in their masses. Others carry metals such as iron, nickel, and cobalt. Certain asteroids contain metals such as titanium and manganese. Future space missions may involve mining asteroids for their valuable resources.

In 1991 the Galileo spacecraft was passing through the asteroid belt on its way to a rendezvous with Jupiter. It captured the first close-up images of an asteroid named Gaspra. The spacecraft encountered a second asteroid, Ida, in August 1993. (See photo.)

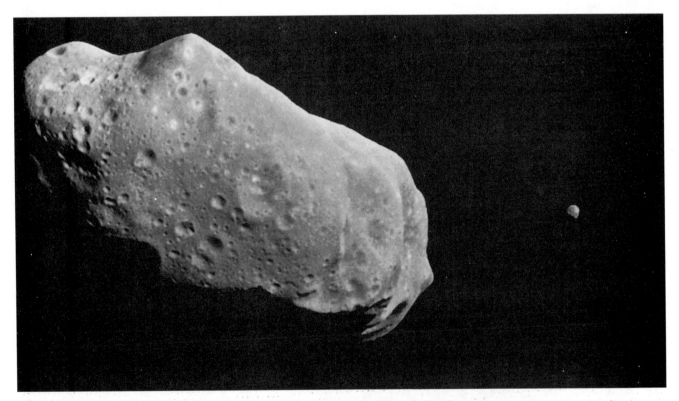

*This image shows both Ida, which is about 56 km (35 mi.) long, and its newly discovered moon—the first conclusive evidence that asteroids can have natural satellites. From this angle, the moon is about 1.5 km (less than 1 mi.) across and is slightly closer to the spacecraft than Ida. The moon has yet to be given a name, but for now it is called "1993 (243) 1." (The numbers denote the year the picture was taken, Ida's asteroid number, and the fact that this is Ida's first discovered moon.)*

# The Asteroid Belt

Most asteroids are also referred to as minor planets or planetoids. They are found in the asteroid belt between the orbits of Mars and Jupiter. Astronomers used to think the asteroids were the remains of a planet. But their total mass is so small, and differences in their composition are so great, that astronomers have rejected this theory.

If asteroids are in the asteroid belt, why are we worried about the possibility of an asteroid impact with Earth? Some asteroids are rebels. The gravitational fields of Jupiter and sometimes Mars disturbs the normal orbits of some of the asteroids, sending them careening into the inner solar system. Some fall into new orbits that cross the orbit of Mars. These are called Amor asteroids. Others, called Apollo asteroids, cross the path of Earth. In this unit you will learn more about some of the near-Earth misses, some of the hits from the past, and our concerns about future impacts.

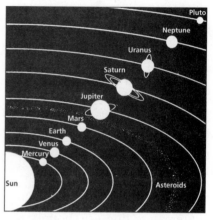

**The asteroid belt (distances are not to scale)**

# Meteoroids, Meteors, and Meteorites

**This stony iron meteor weighs 40 pounds.**

A *meteoroid* is a small piece of debris that orbits the Sun. Meteoroids are formed when a comet or asteroid disintegrates. These fragments have the potential to become *meteors*.

A *meteor*—known as a shooting star by the casual skywatcher—is a fragment of a comet or asteroid that has strayed close enough to Earth to be grabbed by our gravity, then ignited by friction in our atmosphere. A meteor meets its fiery end as a streak of light in the night sky.

Meteor showers, the Leonids every November and the Perseids each August, present light shows worth staying up for on a clear night.

A *meteorite* is the term for a meteor that is large enough to survive this fiery plunge and impact the surface of Earth.

# NIGHT OF SHOOTING STARS

The Earth's passage through the Perseid meteor stream tonight could create a spectacular storm producing thousands of shooting stars per minute: Tonight's forecast, 12A

**Typical meteor**

| Size | From a grain of sand to a pea |
|---|---|
| Speed | Up to 134,000 mph |
| Density | Like balsa wood |

**Where to look**

| Direction | Northeast |
|---|---|
| Best viewing | Along East Coast |
| Peak | Around 9 p.m. ET |

Earth passes through belt of cometary debris. Particles are vaporized 40 to 80 miles above Earth as they enter atmosphere.

Densest part of stream

40,000 miles

Sun

Moon   Earth

Earth's orbit

**Swift-Tuttle comet**
6-mile wide ball of ice and dust passes the Earth's orbit about every 130 years, leaving behind a belt of debris. The shower's intensity is determined by where Earth crosses the stream.

Perseid meteor stream

Comet tail always points away from sun.

Source:
Joe Rao. Compu-Weather Inc.;
Sky & Telescope magazine;
American Astronomical Society

*USA TODAY, AUGUST 11, 1993*

The three varieties of meteorites are: stony, iron, and stony-iron. Stony meteorites are composed of stone or rock similar to rocks on Earth. Iron meteorites are mostly iron and nickel. Stony-iron meteorites are a mix of both.

Meteorites can be found all over our planet. More than 2,500 sites are known. Scientists have even found meteorites that are pieces of the Moon and Mars. The final destination of one large Moon meteorite weighing just under 680 grams (1.5 pounds) was Antarctica. Pieces of Mars dating back to 1,300 million years ago have also been found there.

In addition to meteorites, *tektites* have been found in areas called *strewn fields* found in West Africa, Europe, North America, and in the greatest numbers in the Australian-Asian region. Tektites are small, pitted, glassy objects, usually black, dark green, or amber. They are created when a large meteorite hits Earth in a sandy area. The heat of the impact melts the sand and sends molten globules of it flying into the air. Then they shower down on the terrain.

On the Moon, much of this glassy material can be found in the rays that radiate from impact craters. This debris is called *ejecta* because it has been ejected from the crater site.

# Did an Asteroid Impact End the Dinosaur Age?

Although scientists cannot entirely agree on a theory to explain the disappearance of dinosaurs, the time—65 million years ago—seems uncontested. One explanation is that a "big bang" asteroid impact altered the climate, eliminating the food supply as dust-darkened skies and temperatures cooled.

Some scientists think the effects of this event ricocheted up and down the food chain, blighting the chance for survival for all land animals but sparing those living underground.

Scientists searching for an impact site large enough to have caused such disruption currently favor a recently discovered ancient crater on the Yucatan Peninsula in Mexico.

Pieces of the puzzle await further research.

## IN THE NEWS

**ASTEROID NEAR-HIT:** A two-mile-wide asteroid whizzed near the Earth at midnight, missing by 2.2 million miles. Astronomers say a direct hit by the asteroid Toutatis could be catastrophic. Toutatis passes every four years. By the year 2004 it's expected to pass within 1 million miles — four times the distance between Earth and moon.

**SPACE PHOTOS:** NASA scientists got their best look yet at the kind of object that may have wiped out the dinosaurs and someday could threaten humanity when they took radar pictures of the asteroid Toutatis, which flew close to Earth last month. The new photographs are 100 times more detailed than the best previous images of Earth-approaching asteroids, astronomer Steven Ostro said.

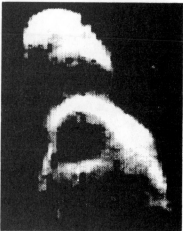

USA TODAY, JANUARY 4, 1993

NASA via AP

**TOUTATIS:** Two-chunk asteroid flew close to Earth.

NASA ARTWORK BY DONALD E. DAVIS

# Asteroid!

The time is two years in the future. It has been reported that a large object (two miles across) is on a collision course with Earth. The threat is real! The people of the world have only a short time to react.

The word *disaster* is derived from Latin words meaning "bad star." The threat of a "bad star" hitting Earth is no laughing matter. In the past, some asteroids have narrowly missed Earth; others have crashed to the ground causing great damage. The new impact could bring upon us the same fate that some scientists think destroyed the dinosaurs—blotting out the Sun, breaking the food chain, and causing massive tsunamis and volcanic eruptions.

A public relations company is working for the newly created United Nations' *Asteroid Awareness Education Committee* (AAEC). The mission of the AAEC is to inform citizens of Earth about the risks of an asteroid or comet collision with Earth. You are part of a team selected by the public relations company. Your job is to produce a multimedia information campaign to meet the goals of the AAEC.

Hardly anyone seems to be taking the collision seriously. After all, there is no record of people being killed by an object falling to Earth from outer space. The public can relate to natural disasters such as floods, earthquakes, volcanic eruptions, and hurricanes. These catastrophic events cause billions of dollars in damage, kill thousands of people, and disrupt society over large areas.

The AAEC needs to make people aware that the impact of an asteroid could cause death and destruction far worse than these other disasters. Campaign materials should be eye catching, creative, and accurate.

You will be presenting important information to the public—increasing people's awareness of the seriousness of this problem so they can participate more actively in its solution. Use as much technology, color, humor, graphics and three-dimensional layouts as you can pack into your multimedia presentation. Never before has your ability to communicate with the public been so crucial. As scientists and public

➤ continued on page 8

---

I saw the meteor at the football game, too. It didn't look too close though, so we weren't frightened. I also saw three other shooting stars when I was in New Hampshire last summer. We had heard about the meteor shower on the news, so my uncle and I went out to watch. We waited for about an hour before we saw the first one. One was green, one was red, and the other was white. I asked my uncle if they could hit us. He said they were too far away. I think that if a big asteroid hit Earth it might make Earth cooler and destroy plant life. But we might be able to shoot missiles at it and break it up.

ASHLEY WOCHHOLZ
DARNESTOWN, MARYLAND

▶ continued from page 7

relations experts, you hold the key to the survival of civilization as we know it.

With your team, decide on a catchy name for the ad firm. Design a logo for the firm and a business card for the members of your team. Give the business cards to your teacher.

Science activities in this module only provide some of the pieces that will make up your final product. What is missing is the creation of the final information campaign. Remember, the final product must use a *multimedia* approach to educating the public. The activities will give you the basis for a print campaign, but you must add either television, radio, or both. The design for the final campaign is up to you and the rest of your team. The Public Relations Manager will assign jobs and coordinate the campaign.

IMPORTANT: As you brainstorm ideas for the final campaign, make sure you assign roles to match the strengths and motivation of each member of your team. Also, do not plan a television campaign unless you have access to the necessary equipment.

## Choosing Your Expert Role

You and your team members will each submit a prioritized list to your teacher with your role preferences (first choice, and so on). First choices will be assigned if possible.

Before you decide on your preferred role, read over the Expert Task descriptions and make sure you are willing and able to meet the responsibilities of the role.

## Expert Tasks

**Public Relations Manager/Team Coordinator:** Coordinate the development of a logo for the AAEC public relations team, coordinate the final information campaign, and be responsible for collecting and storing all group-designed items. You will need very good communication skills.

**Planetary Scientist:** Lead a team discussion of the Orbit Logo activity, and use resulting data to develop visuals that convince the public that the asteroid threat is real.

**Paleontologist:** Lead a team discussion of the Time After Time activity, and use resulting data on

mass-extinction events and approximate dates of prehistoric asteroid impacts to create convincing graphics and slogans for the team's information campaign.

**Physicist:** Lead a team discussion of the Crater Creator activity, and use resulting information about the physics of crater formation to create convincing graphics and slogans for the team's information campaign.

**Amateur Astronomer:** Lead a team discussion of the Solar System Business Guide activity, and use resulting data about the Sun, planets, satellites, comets, and asteroids to create graphics, posters, scripts, and whatever else is needed to support your team's information campaign.

IMPORTANT: Each member of your team will develop a fictitious business suitable for one specific location in the solar system and assist the team coordinator with the final information campaign.■

# Public Relations Manager

BETH WILLIAMS
SPACE MARKETING, INC.
ROSWELL, GEORGIA

As president of Space Marketing, Inc., I am keenly interested in educating the public concerning the commercial use of outer space.

I think space has to start marketing itself. The world is more sophisticated now than when we landed the first humans on the Moon back in 1969. I firmly believe that the public, at a grassroots level, is very interested in the future of space exploration. To the average person, it is a fascinating subject.

One way to attract more interest in space is through advertising. For instance, to promote a new motion picture, Columbia Pictures hired Space Marketing to design an ad for the side of a rocket called Conestoga. We're looking at other innovative advertising ideas, such as launching flour on a recoverable spacecraft and then using it to make batches of "space chips." Another idea proposed by a newspaper is to launch ink into space, then recover the ink to print a special publication on space exploration.

We've got lots of ideas . . . even on how to sell the colonization of the Moon!

We're not in favor of polluting or harming the atmosphere. I do not support placing billboards in space that you would see 24 hours a day, day after day.

Our latest venture is working with the Lunar and Planetary Institute in Houston, Texas. We are helping the scientists there raise money to explore the Chicxulub Basin in northernmost Yucatan, Mexico. As you may know, this basin is the largest and best preserved of the craters now known on Earth. Thought to be formed by the impact of an asteroid or comet 65 million years ago, the crater may be as wide as 190 miles across.

We are seeking financial assistance from corporations to help explore the site. We hope to be able to determine whether or not the Chicxulub crater was the big event that led to the extinction of dinosaurs and much of life on Earth 65 million years ago.

Marketing is different from being an engineer. While you must have good common sense and the ability to think on your feet, you also need a head for business and numbers.

To those interested in marketing, I recommend getting a good, overall liberal arts education. Being able to mix well with people from all backgrounds is also a must. No matter what you are marketing, it certainly helps to have a real devotion and love of the product or subject. In marketing space, knowing the "space basics" is important. However, you don't need to know every scientific detail.

If an asteroid or comet were headed toward Earth, the most important thing to know is whether or not it will actually hit us. Certainly, if we know an object is going to strike Earth, we need to start planning and anticipate the catastrophe. Do we have time to move people out of an area? How big is the asteroid and how much destruction might be caused? What companies can be called on to help with disaster relief by donating food and other supplies?

These considerations must be addressed when planning a campaign to educate the public about the impending disaster. On the other hand, if the asteroid passes us by, you might have a lot of fun with advertising. How about a "name the asteroid" contest, with scholarships provided by big-name companies?

Space marketing is absolutely unlimited. Today, frankly, many people have a lot to worry about, so space sometimes offers a diversion.

# Crater Creator

## Purpose

To investigate how an "asteroid's" speed and size affect the diameter of an impact crater.

## Materials

**For each group:**
- "Asteroids" (marbles, plastic beads, BBs, or small pebbles of various diameters and masses)
- Meter stick
- Sand (enough for 6-cm depth in container)
- Shallow container (such as a shoe box)
- Clamps
- Ring stand
- Metric ruler
- Balance
- Watch or clock with second hand

**For each student:**
- Pencil
- Metric ruler
- Paper

## Activity

Background: News is spreading! People are full of questions about the shocking report that a renegade asteroid is heading for a collision with Earth. You are employed by an advertising agency working for the United Nations' *Asteroid Awareness Education Committee* (AAEC). The AAEC has asked you to design an experiment that elementary school students can conduct. They intend to publish your experiment in *Science and Children*™, a journal of the National Science Teachers Association. You see this as an opportunity to use news reports to get students interested in the study of astronomy.

Students have probably already heard the reports. An asteroid missed Earth by 500,000 miles in 1989. In 1991 a 30-foot-wide asteroid shot past Earth at a distance half as close as the Moon. In May 1993 an asteroid came within 90,000 miles of Earth, and it was only spotted after it had passed us! The mass of that asteroid was estimated to be 6,000 tons. Now, reports of a killer asteroid have caught the attention of the entire world. This one will not miss!

You predict that students will ask some of the following questions: Where will it hit? How big is it? How fast is it going? Is it true that dinosaurs were wiped out by an asteroid? When will this one hit? Do big asteroids make larger craters than small asteroids? Does the speed of the asteroid have anything to do with crater size?

You have decided to design an experiment that will help students answer the last two of these questions: How does the *speed* of the asteroid affect the diameter of its crater? How does the *size* of an asteroid affect a diameter of its crater? You need to:

1. Design the experiment so that a variety of samples is tested. Be sure your procedures address the questions you want answered. Write up the procedure for experiment.
2. Draw and label an illustration showing students how to set up any needed equipment.
3. Conduct the experiment yourself. Make necessary additions or corrections to your procedure so all questions are addressed. Keep careful notes.
4. Organize data into an appropriate data table.

These steps will make it easier for you to compare your results to the data other investigators collect.

## Conclusion

You have designed an experiment, tested and revised it, and obtained some sample results. You are now ready to prepare final copy to send to teachers for use with their students. You must provide teachers with the following:

1. A neatly prepared copy of your experimental procedure.
2. A neatly prepared diagram of your equipment setup.
3. A blank data table their students can use to record their results.
4. A summary of your findings.
5. Suggestions to the teacher.
6. Optional: A photograph of a student conducting the experiment or a graph showing typical data.

# Definitions

### Mass and Density

The *mass* of an object is the total amount of matter contained within it. The *density* of an object is a measure of how tightly packed the matter is, or the quantity of mass per unit of volume.

### Gravity

All objects having mass exert an inward, attractive gravitational force on all other objects having mass. The greater the mass of an object, the stronger its gravitational pull. Objects as small as an atom or as large as a galaxy exert the force known as the *pull of gravity*.

### Black Holes

Astronomers use the term *black hole* to describe a region of space where the pull of gravity is so great that nothing, not even light, can escape. In the final stages of a star's evolution, a very massive star exhausts its supply of natural atomic fuel. One possible fate is for it to become a black hole.

As the star burns out, the resulting lack of internal pressure causes the gravity of the star to collapse the core remnant into itself with great violence. The remaining entity then has near zero volume, but almost infinite gravity. In this bizarre final phase of star evolution, the resulting "object" emits no light and no radiation, but anything that passes close enough plunges into the black hole never to be seen again.

# NEAR Mission and Clementine

Just a few years ago, people wondered what an asteroid would even look like. Thanks to spacecraft, we now have close-up views of several asteroids, and we are charting even more daring encounters with these mini-worlds in years to come.

The U.S. *Galileo* spacecraft, en route to its 1995 rendezvous with Jupiter, was on a course that permitted it to fly by two of the celestial clumps: asteroid Gaspra in October 1991 and asteroid Ida in August 1993.

Scheduled for launch in February 1996, the Near Earth Asteroid Rendezvous (NEAR) spacecraft will attempt to set a new milestone in space research: It will orbit an asteroid. The target of the NEAR mission is asteroid Eros, one of the best-known and largest of near-Earth crossing asteroids. Eros is an unevenly shaped asteroid that is 36 kilometers (22 miles) wide at one point. NEAR will orbit the asteroid for up to a year beginning in December 1998. Carrying a camera and a host of other instruments, it can conduct intensive studies of Eros at very close range.

*This picture of asteroid 951 Gaspra is a mosaic of two images taken by the Galileo spacecraft from a range of 3,300 miles about 10 minutes before its closest approach to Earth on October 29, 1991.*

# What Is a Comet?

A tiny pearl of light races across our solar system with a luminous tail of dust. What is this bewildering phenomena that frightened people in centuries past?

It is called a comet—sometimes it is referred to as a "dirty snowball." Its solid nucleus is composed of tiny particles of rock, dust, water vapor, and frozen gases. A comet passes through the solar system on a highly elliptical (egg-shaped) orbit. As it nears the Sun, the outer ices of the head of the comet are converted by solar heat into vapor, thus releasing particles of dust. These are repelled by the solar wind, creating a bright tail that may stream out into space for millions of miles.

As a comet travels its path around the Sun, the solar wind (the outward flow of charged particles from the Sun) causes the tail to point away from the Sun. As a comet approaches, its head leads the way into the "wind" and the tail streams out behind; but as its orbit carries the comet past the Sun, the tail slowly swings around, always pointing away

*Comet Ikeya-Seki*

from the Sun. Once the comet embarks on its path away from the Sun, the tail takes the lead. Some comets travel their oval orbit in less than 7 years, while others make huge orbits, nearing the Sun only once in thousands or millions of years.

Astronomers have given the more famous comets specific names. Best known is Halley's Comet, first observed before A.D. 240. It was named for the English astronomer Edmond Halley. Halley discovered that the comet could be observed every 76 years as it orbited the Sun. Two such orbits were recorded during the twentieth century—in 1910 and in 1986. Halley's Comet will return in 2061. How old will you be then?

Bright comets can be recorded on film even by amateur photographers. All you need are a good camera, a tripod, fast film, and time-exposure patience.

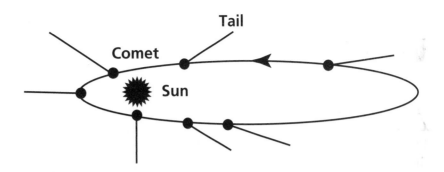

*This digital computer enhancement of Comet Halley in 1985 shows the comet when it was 67.6 million miles from Earth and the tail was 3 million miles long. The image shows the brightness contour levels of the coma.*

# Physicist

**DR. PHILIP MORRISON
INSTITUTE PROFESSOR
EMERITUS
MASSACHUSETTS INSTITUTE
OF TECHNOLOGY
CAMBRIDGE, MASSACHUSETTS**

On my fifth birthday, it just so happened that the first ordinary radio broadcast took place in the United States. That's when I became interested in science.

We lived near the Westinghouse plant in Pennsylvania where that first transmission was made. For several weeks before the broadcast, various downtown stores began to sell small crystal radio sets. My father always liked new things and brought home a radio. I was captivated by it and never looked back.

I became an amateur radio operator at an early age. Of course, I did all the usual things while I was a school kid—chemistry, explosives, and magic. But my central interest was in radio. So I wanted to go to college and become a radio engineer.

The college had to be close because it was during the depression and times were tough for everyone. I was very lucky—just a mile away was an excellent engineering school now called Carnegie-Mellon University, in Pittsburgh,Pennsylvania.

In college I met electrical engineers and physicists. Engineers seemed far too careful, while most physicists were more open-minded and curious. Being more interested in the imaginative style of physicists, I

became one.

I was a nuclear physicist during World War II. Shortly after that, my interest in cosmic rays led me to astronomy. For the last 30 to 40 years, I have mainly been involved in astronomy with considerable interest in radio astronomy.

Throughout my life, I have been interested in magic. Magic—conjuring or stage magic—is very close to theoretical physics because you have to understand what people think is going on; then you know what is really going on and you can manipulate it to blur that edge. It's very instructive. I still go to watch the magicians. I like to talk with them about what they do.

My advice to students is that you can't have too much mathematics and science. On the other hand, you have to know a lot of other things as well. So become interested in something. It doesn't matter much what you do, as long as you do it well and make a contribution.

When it comes to mathematics, remember that big and small are different, and estimating is important. Times tables are important but you can do so much better with a four-function calculator. The main thing is to have an understanding of mathematics and be able to estimate.

Science is all around us. It helps us understand what is happening not only when watching the sky, but in the kitchen too.

I do a lot of cooking. I can't cook without observing and experimenting. Did you know that the size you cut the food determines how fast it cooks? What you do in the kitchen is scientific all the way.

The same thing is true in looking at the evening sky. I'm a naked-eye astronomer. You don't have to have a telescope at all. You can just watch the things that happen.

Science is a way of understanding the natural world as well as the artificial world we are creating. You can see the design of everything and how it works. When something goes wrong, science can help you understand what happened.

This is the case with an asteroid impacting Earth. Educating the public about asteroids would involve several things. One might show people the many impact craters on Earth including the meteor crater in Arizona. It is absolutely conspicuous!

Then I would use films, models, and maps comparing the Arizona crater with craters on the Moon. Clearly the Moon has been bombarded by asteroids and comets. There is hardly any of the Moon left that is not cratered.

Earth's weathering and internal processes have covered up most of the craters on our planet. Now we only find vague, circular traces, like Hudson Bay.

But the solar system is still full of loose objects. One of these leftovers could strike on land or sea. To educate the public about such a possibility, you need to discuss such an event using the scale of the energy released. Compare an asteroid impact with other natural events such as hurricanes and earthquakes.

**Meteor crater in Arizona**

If an asteroid collision with Earth is eminent, all forms of media must be used. This is a world-wide problem. Keep in mind that different countries use different forms of mass communications. What might be most effective in one country might not work in another.

Furthermore, there is need to decentralize the communications

used. A mobilization of many people around the world is needed, be they newspaper writers, teachers, editors, or even disc jockeys.

One of the most serious effects from an asteroid impact concerns the atmosphere. The impact would cause a general change in the chemistry of the atmosphere. High temperatures caused by the asteroid's shock wave would create enormous amounts of nitric oxides in the atmosphere. That would lead to a rain of nitric acid fouling the land and our oceans.

The prospect of Earth being hit by a celestial object doesn't seem remote to the public any more. Since Jupiter was hit by pieces of a comet in July 1994 the threat to us has become more real.

**DISCOVERY FILE**

# Jupiter and the Sun: The Double-Star System Theory

Our solar system revolves around a single star, the Sun. As common as it seems to us, the single-star system is not typical. The majority of stars throughout the universe are members of two-star systems, called *binary-star systems.*

In binary systems, two stars, held together by their mutual gravitational attraction, orbit around a common center of mass, often a point between the two of them. Many other stars are companions in triple,

quadruple, and even more complex star systems, such as star clusters.

During the formation of our solar system, was the giant planet Jupiter marked for stardom? Jupiter is similar in composition to the stars; it is primarily hydrogen and helium with traces of the heavier elements. Why didn't Jupiter form into a star?

In the early history of our solar system, Jupiter was much larger and hotter. Since that time, it has cooled and reduced

in size to where its central temperature is much too low to activate the nuclear furnace that energizes even a small, dim star. Jupiter would have to be 80 times more massive for its central temperature to increase to the level needed for nuclear fusion reactions.

If Jupiter had been big enough to become a star, our planetary neighborhood would be very different today. Most likely, life as we know it would not have taken up residence on planet Earth.

# Scientific Sleuthing

One of the great puzzles in history is why the dinosaurs became extinct. Before exploring the theories about this extinction, consider first the history of Earth. The sweep of geologic time is divided and subdivided into distinct units, just as we carve up the time today into days, weeks, months, years, decades, and centuries.

Dinosaurs appear to have emerged during the Triassic period more than 200 million years ago. Following the Triassic period is the Jurassic period, which lasted about 45 million years. As movie director Stephen Spielberg captured in his film *Jurassic Park,* this was the time when dinosaurs dominated Earth. After the Jurassic period came the Cretaceous period. It ended about 65 million years ago. It was at the end of this stretch of time that dinosaurs became extinct. But why? This is the great puzzle.

Time has erased most evidence for the cause of the extinction. Dinosaurs may have died a slow death, their numbers dwindling gradually over thousands of years, or something catastrophic could have killed them all in a day or two. All we know is that the fossil record for dinosaurs dramatically and abruptly ends.

For many years, scientists have wondered what could have snuffed out the dinosaurs. One theory is that the climate changed enough to kill them; another theory blames a plague or disease. Some scientists have speculated that plant life was altered somehow, causing dietary problems in plant-eating dinosaurs and eventually leading to the extinction of the meat-eaters. An exploding star (a supernova) has also been posed as reasons for the extinction. Lethal doses of radiation cascading to Earth from such a failed star might cause mass extinctions by triggering climate changes and making Earth unsuitable for life.

Although each of these ideas has merits, each also has weaknesses. One of the more provocative theories today points to another possibility—perhaps the dinosaurs died in a single, massive, and catastrophic event 65 million years ago: perhaps a 6-mile-wide asteroid hit Earth!

I was in Nags Head, North Carolina, last August during the meteor shower. My friend and I were on the beach looking at the stars, when all of a sudden people behind us yelled, "Look at that!" I turned in time to see a meteor skipping across the sky. It appeared to have a tail like a comet but much brighter and bigger. It lasted only five seconds. We were lucky enough to see a few more meteors before we went in, but the first one was the biggest.

Later I found out that this particular meteor shower had more meteors than usual because Earth was passing through a concentration of comet debris. Some of the "fireballs" looked huge, but most were really no bigger than grains of sand.

MATTHEW TOOMEY
POOLESVILLE, MARYLAND

What proof do we have for an asteroid impact wiping out the dinosaurs? You could call it extraterrestrial fingerprints. This is the evidence put forth by the father and son team of Luis Alvarez, Nobel Prize-winning physicist, and Walter Alvarez, a geologist. Starting in the late 1970s, the team discovered that concentrated amounts of iridium (a rare element more commonly found in meteorites) can be detected in a layer of clay in Earth's crust. More importantly, this thin layer of clay containing the iridium deposit marks the boundary between the end of the Cretaceous era (K)—when dinosaurs roamed Earth and then vanished—and the beginning of the new age, the Tertiary (T) period.

The scientific sleuths found similar concentrations of iridium in the K-T boundary on a worldwide basis. One by one, possible sources for the iridium deposit were rejected by the Alvarez team. They were left with one plausible delivery route: it came from inside the solar system. Their theory was that Earth had been struck by a hefty-sized asteroid or comet, a "terminator rock" as it has been called. The environment of our planet was a casualty. Nearly 75 percent of life on the globe became extinct, including the dinosaurs who had lorded over Earth for 150 million years.

The Yucatan peninsula of Mexico has been singled out as the spot where an extraterrestrial object struck Earth and possibly triggered the mass extinction. The Yucatan impact crater, at a site called Chicxulub on the north coast of the peninsula, is more than 180 miles wide and is now buried beneath about 2 miles of sediment. Debris from the impact has been found at many sites in the Caribbean and the region around the Gulf of Mexico, as well as in the western United States. ■

IN THE NEWS

# Did the dinosaurs suffocate?

By Tim Friend
USA TODAY

The end of the dinosaur era was marked by a rapid decline in atmospheric oxygen — creating an environment in which wheezing giants roamed, too tired to compete, a new theory says.

"If you're chasing down dinner and pass out before you get to eat, that would not enhance survivability," says Gary Landis, U.S. Geological Survey in Boulder, Colo.

Researchers analyzed ancient gas bubbles trapped in amber. Results, reported Wednesday at the Geological Society of America meeting, shows oxygen levels declined rapidly before the dinosaurs disappeared.

Why did the decline occur so fast? Landis and his colleagues say the air was rich with oxygen because volcanic activity pumped out carbon dioxide, which was converted to oxygen by plants.

When the volcanic "super plumes" shut down, carbon levels fell, plant life declined and oxygen levels dropped.

That seems to have happened over 6 million years about 65 million years ago.

The main competing dinosaur theory: They died after an asteroid hit the Earth and dust clouds blocked the sun.

USA TODAY, 1993

# Scientists Explain 1908 Tunguska Mystery

In early 1993 three U.S. scientists claimed they solved the mystery of the explosion that devastated a Siberian forest in 1908. Using a mathematical simulation of the Tunguska explosion and a bit of logic, they proposed that a 100-foot to 200-foot stony asteroid caused the explosion.

The asteroid is believed to have vaporized 8 kilometers (5 miles) above the Siberian forest. The blast laid waste 2,000 square kilometers (1,243 square miles) with a force of 12 million tons of the powerful explosive TNT; this would be 800 times more powerful than the atomic bomb dropped on Hiroshima.

The shock waves of the explosion tossed a man 7 feet even though he was standing 65 kilometers (40 miles) away. It also set fires for miles around.

The explosion had remained a mystery for so many years because the only thing left of the asteroid after it vaporized were small traces of the chemical element iridium.

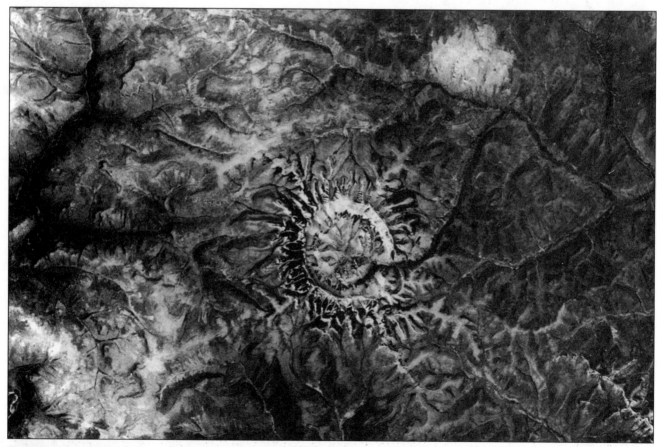

*Gora Konder crater in Russia, photographed by the NASA Space Shuttle*

# Paleontologist

NARDOS FESSAHA
HOWARD UNIVERSITY
WASHINGTON, D.C.

I think it was my interest in the history of life that influenced me to pursue a career in paleontology. I was attracted to paleontology early in my university studies. I wanted to know more about evolution, especially human evolution.

In high school, I was really into biology, and I liked natural history and chemistry as well. My father also encouraged my interest in medical science. Now I am a graduate student in paleontology and anatomy working on my doctorate degree at Howard University in Washington, D.C.

My home is in Ethiopia, Africa. I came to the United States for graduate studies and research. I plan to return to Ethiopia after earning my degree. I would like to do research in paleontology at the National Museum in Ethiopia and participate in expanding the paleontology research program there.

But for now I have my graduate studies. I teach an anatomy laboratory class at Howard University, and I am involved in an exciting research project. You may have heard of "Lucy." Lucy is the name of the remains that is possibly one of our ancient ancestors. The remains were found in the archeological excavations of Hadar, Ethiopia.

I am a member of a research team that is studying the animals also found in that area. My specialty is fossil pigs. Other researchers are studying fossil horses, elephants, rhinoceroses, monkeys, mollusks, and plants.

Science enables you to see the importance of the diversity of life—that is why I am interested in science. It's not just your family, or the people close to you, or humanity; it's about all forms of life around you.

Understanding science gives you a larger view of things. As you work on a plan to inform people around the world of the seriousness of an asteroid impact with Earth, you need to consider the difference between countries the size of the United States and smaller countries such as Ethiopia. There is a big difference.

As far as reaching people with the printed word, remember there is much less literacy in smaller, undeveloped countries than in developed countries such as the United States.

Some years ago, there was a literacy campaign in Ethiopia. High school and university students went into local communities to teach reading and writing to the people. But there are still many people who can't read. Written material would not be the best way to reach the most people about the coming asteroid.

Most of the people in Ethiopia live in the country, far away from any form of technology such as television. Some people have radios—so that could be one way to reach part of the population. There aren't that many big cities in Ethiopia, and even in the city, there are few people who would understand an asteroid striking Earth from a scientific perspective. It is unlikely they would be open to the scientific explanation of this possible catastrophe.

So as you develop your plan for reaching people worldwide, be sure to consider cultural and religious beliefs, methods of communication within each country, and availability of related technology.

# Charting the Planets

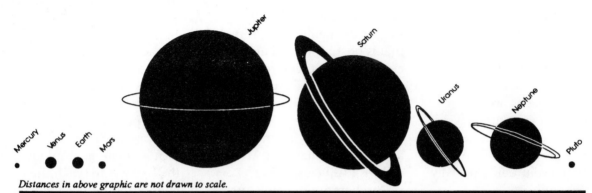

*Distances in above graphic are not drawn to scale.*

| Categories | Mercury | Venus | Earth | Mars | Jupiter | Saturn | Uranus | Neptune | Pluto |
|---|---|---|---|---|---|---|---|---|---|
| 1. Mean Distance From Sun (Millions of Kilometers) | 57.9 | 108.2 | 149.6 | 227.9 | 778.3 | 1,427 | 2,871 | 4,497 | 5,914 |
| 2. Period of Revolution | 88 days | 224.7 days | 365.3 days | 687 days | 11.86 years | 29.46 years | 84 years | 165 years | 248 years |
| 3. Equatorial Diameter (Kilometers) | 4,880 | 12,100 | 12,756 | 6,794 | 143,200 | 120,000 | 51,800 | 49,528 | ~2,330 |
| 4. Atmosphere (Main Components) | Virtually None | Carbon Dioxide | Nitrogen Oxygen | Carbon Dioxide | Hydrogen Helium | Hydrogen Helium | Helium Hydrogen Methane | Hydrogen Helium Methane | Methane + ? |
| 5. Moons | 0 | 0 | 1 | 2 | 16 | 18 | 15 | 8 | 1 |
| 6. Rings | 0 | 0 | 0 | 0 | 3 | 1,000 (?) | 11 | 4 | 0 |
| 7. Inclination of Orbit to Ecliptic | 7° | 3.4° | 0° | 1.9° | 1.3° | 2.5° | 0.8° | 1.8° | 17.1° |
| 8. Eccentricity of Orbit | .206 | .007 | .017 | .093 | .048 | .056 | .046 | .009 | .248 |
| 9. Rotation Period | 59 days | 243 days Retrograde | 23 hours 56 min. | 24 hours 37 min. | 9 hours 55 min. | 10 hours 40 min. | 17.2 hours Retrograde | 16 hours 7 min. | 6 days 9 hours 18 min. Retrograde |
| 10. Inclination of Axis* | Near 0° | 177.2° | 23° 27' | 25° 12' | 3° 5' | 26° 44' | 97° 55' | 28° 48' | 120° |

* Inclinations greater than 90° imply retrograde rotation.

# The Sun

At the center of a swirling cloud of gas, about 4.7 billion years ago, our nearest star—the Sun—was born. Strange as it may seem, the Sun occupies 1 million times the space of our planet. Its diameter is 100 times the diameter of Earth.

The Sun actually contains more than 99 percent of all the matter in our solar system. The two most basic elements in the universe exist in the Sun. The fuel for its great nuclear furnace is hydrogen, which currently constitutes 92 percent of the Sun's volume. Deep within the Sun, pairs of hydrogen atoms are joining together to form single helium atoms.

Helium currently makes up about 7 percent of the Sun's volume. (The word *currently* is used here because as hydrogen fuses to become helium, the proportion of each changes.) The last 1 percent consists of at least 80 of the other 90 natural elements.

The Sun holds the most vital link in our food web. From plankton to people, its life-giving light and warmth are responsible for the survival of all life on Earth.

*This photo, taken December 19, 1993, shows one of the most spectacular solar flares ever recorded.*

# Mercury

Mercury is the Sun's closest neighbor. Its crater-ridden surface resembles our Moon's surface. Mercury was appropriately named for the Roman wing-footed messenger of the gods. It speeds around the Sun at 48 kilometers (30 miles) per second, completing a solar rotation—a Mercurian year—in 88 Earth days.

At about one-third the size of Earth, Mercury is smaller than any other planet except Pluto. However, the density of Mercury is about the same as Earth's, therefore, it is assumed to have an iron core as Earth does.

One theory as to why the density of Mercury is high is that the planet may have been impacted by a large body early in its history. The impact may have ripped off its lighter, outer layers and transformed the planet into a dense, floating island of rock and metal.

*Mercury as seen by the Mariner 10 spacecraft. The incoming and outgoing views are shown.*

# Origin of the Solar System

About 4.7 billion years ago, in the outer spiral arm of what we call the Milky Way Galaxy, a cloud of interstellar matter (mostly hydrogen and dust) collapsed to form our solar system. This catastrophic event may have begun as the result of the explosion of a nearby star.

Gravity radiating from the center of this cloud of gas and dust caused the cloud to contract, or pull in on itself. As it contracted, temperatures and pressures rose so high that a thermonuclear fusion reaction began. Hydrogen atoms fused (joined together with other hydrogen atoms) to form helium—this process created our Sun.

Matter that lay far from the center of mass did not become part of the Sun. It condensed to become the planets, moons, asteroids, and comets that are now the orbital companions of the Sun. As we can observe by exploring the cratered surfaces of many objects in our solar system, this early period was a time of chaotic collisions and mass destruction.

The small moon Miranda, a satellite of Uranus, shows evidence of collisions so large they literally tore Miranda apart. As time passed, Miranda slowly reassembled, displaying a bizarre pattern of surface features. Even our own moon may have been torn from the surface of Earth by a massive impact.

Over billions of years, the gravitational force of the Sun has brought some order to our solar system. Yet, there still remains the threat of asteroids and comets that periodically cross Earth's orbit.

# The Ins and Outs of the Solar System

In contrast to the outer planets, the inner or terrestrial planets are small, close together, and near the Sun. They consist mostly of solid rocky substances and they rotate slowly, have few moons, possess no rings, and show weak or no magnetic fields.

Among these inner planets, Earth is unique. It is the only planet to have free oxygen and liquid water.

The outer planets are large, are widely separated and distant from the Sun, are primarily gaseous, rotate more rapidly, and have strong magnetic fields. Their beauty is enhanced by many moons and colorful rings. Their atmospheres contain mainly helium, hydrogen, methane, and ammonia; terrestrial planets have atmospheres consisting mostly of carbon dioxide and nitrogen.

All planets revolve around the Sun in the same direction and in nearly the same plane. Each planet rotates on an axis as it travels its orbit.

Pluto, the smallest of the outer planets and usually most distant from the Sun, is not gaseous. It resembles the icy moons of some of the outer planets.

*The solar system's four largest planets are compared with Earth in this photomontage. Unlike Earth, these giant worlds are composed primarily of hydrogen and helium.*

# Time After Time

## Purpose

To use a time line to compare mass extinctions with asteroid impacts.

## Materials

- Adding machine tape
- Meter stick
- Scissors
- Colored pencils
- Geologic Time Chart (page 24)
- Mass Extinction Time Line (page 24)
- Asteroid Impact Time Line (page 24)
- Hole punch
- Earth science texts, paleontology books, and encyclopedias

## Activity

Background: The Asteroid Awareness Education Committee (AAEC) is concerned that people are not taking the impending asteroid impact seriously enough.

The AAEC has contracted your company to design an educational display that can be placed on the sides of trucks and buses, and on the inside of subway cars. They want the display to show the relationship (if any exists) between past asteroid impacts and mass extinctions. You and your partner(s) are the scientists who must decide if such a relationship exists. If it does, the design department will take over. If no relationship exists, the AAEC will have to find another way to scare the public into paying attention.

Scientists have determined that Earth is about 4.5 billion years old. That's the same as 4,000 million years plus another 500 million years! Using numbers like *thousands* and *millions* when talking about years is cumbersome. It also has little meaning for most people. The farther back in time you go, or the greater the number of years, the harder it is for us to understand. So scientists use other markers to place events in an appropriate time frame. The geologic time scale divides our past into three units of time based on observable changes in the fossil record. The largest unit is *era*. Eras are subdivided into *periods*, and periods are further divided into *epochs*.

Placing events on this type of time scale is easy. Look at the Geologic Time Chart at the end of this activity. Dinosaurs became extinct at the end of the last part of the Mesozoic Era, just before the Cenozoic Era. More precisely, they became extinct between the Cretaceous Period (abbreviated K) and the Tertiary Period (abbreviated T). The boundary between the Cretaceous and Tertiary Periods is often called the K-T boundary.

It is known that at least six mass extinctions of plants and animals have occurred over the last 570 million years. Exactly why particular mass extinctions occurred is hotly disputed. As new discoveries are made, scientists modify their hypotheses and theories to explain the events they observe. Theories about mass extinctions have included:

- Changing climates
- Volcanic activity
- Overpopulation
- Rising and falling sea levels
- Shifting continents
- Widespread disease
- Asteroid impacts
- All or some of the above happening at the same time.

There are data that support most of these theories in whole or in part. Making a decision about which theory to support (if any) can be hard, but that is just what the AAEC wants you to do. Since an asteroid is about to strike Earth, they have asked you to explore the idea that asteroids may have caused mass extinctions in the past. After your examination of the data, present your findings in a memorandum to the AAEC.

1. Measure and cut 4.5 meters of adding machine tape.
2. Study the Geologic Time Chart (on page 24), then decide on an appropriate scale for the tape. Divide your tape into appropriate time units.
3. Label all eras, periods, and epochs in order, at their proper places on the adding machine tape.
4. Decorate your time line with drawings of animal and plant life from the various times. Use texts and encyclopedias as references for your drawings.
5. Decide on graphic representations for mass extinctions. Draw them on your time line at appropriate times.

➤ continued on page 24

➤ continued from page 23

6. Punch holes in your time line to indicate major asteroid impacts.

Think about these questions as you write a memorandum to the AAEC:

- Compare the Precambrian Era to the rest of the time chart. What percentage of the total geologic time does it represent?
- According to the data on your chart, what is the average length of time between mass extinctions?
- What is the average time between major impacts?
- Is there a correlation between major impacts and mass extinctions? Where on the time chart can you find a correlation?
- Is there a way to predict the year in which the next large impact might occur? Support your answer with facts from your time line.

## Mass Extinctions Through Geologic Time

| Millions of Years Ago | Geologic Period | Life Forms Affected |
| --- | --- | --- |
| .01 | Quaternary | Large mammals and birds |
| 66 | Cretaceous | Dinosaurs, foraminifera, mollusks, ammonites—up to 75 percent of species died out during this time |
| 200 | Triassic | Many reptiles and ammonoids—35 percent of all animal families |
| 250 | Permian | Many trees, amphibians, most bryozoans, brachiopods, all trilobites, 50 percent of all animal families, over 95 percent of all marine species |
| 360 | Devonian | Agnathan and placoderm fish, many trilobites, 30 percent of all animal families |
| 500 | Cambrian | Most trilobites, 50 percent of all animal species |

Note: Significant extinctions occurred at the boundaries between periods. These boundaries are well defined by fossils called *index fossils,* many of which became extinct at the end of the period.

## Geologic Time Chart

| ERA | PERIOD | EPOCH | BEGAN-Millions of years ago |
| --- | --- | --- | --- |
| CENOZOIC | Quaternary | Holocene | 0.001 |
| | | Pleistocene | 1.8 |
| | Tertiary | Pliocene | 5.5 |
| | | Miocene | 22.0 |
| | | Oligocene | 35.0 |
| | | Eocene | 50.0 |
| | | Paleocene | 65.0 |
| MESOZOIC | Cretaceous | | 135.0 |
| | Jurassic | | 190.0 |
| | Triassic | | 225.0 |
| PALEOZOIC | Permian | | 280.0 |
| | Pennsylvanian | | 325.0 |
| | Missipian | | 345.0 |
| | Devonian | | 395.0 |
| | Siluran | | 430.0 |
| | Ordovician | | 500.0 |
| | Cambrian | | 570.0 |
| | Precambrian (Phanerozoic) Era | | 4,500.0 |

## Major Known Impacts Throughout Geologic History

(Craters with a diameter of 30 kilometers or greater)

| Location | Diam. (km) | Age (millions of years) |
| --- | --- | --- |
| Canada | 30 | 350 |
| Canada | 32 | 290 |
| USA, Iowa | 32 | 70 |
| Canada | 37 | 485 |
| Brazil | 40 | 250 |
| Canada | 46 | 360 |
| Russia | 50 | 57 |
| Sweden | 52 | 365 |
| Canada | 70 | 210 |
| Russia | 80 | 183 |
| Russia | 100 | 39 |
| Canada | 140 | 1,840 |
| South Africa | 140 | 1,970 |
| Mexico | 300 | 65 |

Based on work by R.A.F. Grieve published in *Geological Society of America Special Paper No. 190* (1982). Ages of impact craters are approximate. Errors range from 1 percent to 10 percent.

# Heavenly Visitors

A dramatic incident took place on June 30, 1908. High over Tunguska, Siberia, a 100-foot to 200-foot (30-meter to 60-meter) diameter celestial object exploded, releasing the energy force of a 10-megaton to 20-megaton bomb. Scientists still debate whether the projectile was an asteroid or a small comet. An asteroid is believed more likely. Whatever it was, the space invader flattened 2,000 square kilometers of forest, apparently setting forested areas ablaze. The powerful Tunguska blast released pressure waves that jangled meteorological barographs in distant England.

Should a similar event happen today over a densely-populated area, hundreds of thousands of people would be instantly killed. Buildings would be flattened over a 20-kilometer radius. Property damage would be measured in hundreds of billions of dollars.

In fact, cosmic collisions between Earth and objects from space are more common than you think. The great majority of meteorites are fragments of asteroids. Hundreds of kilograms of meteoric material filter down daily through Earth's atmosphere. These tiny grains and fine dust are the by-products of small meteorites diving through and disintegrating in the upper atmosphere.

Every few days, fragments from a larger-sized meteorite survive the 45,000-mile-per-hour entry into the atmosphere. The remaining pieces land on Earth's surface. These meteorites usually plunge into ocean waters and other deserted places, never to be recovered—but not always.

On October 9, 1992, a high school senior heard what sounded like a three-car crash outside her Peekskill, New York, apartment. When she went

➤ continued on page 26

---

It was a summer day in Mazatlan, Mexico, in the year 1991. The Sun was bright, the kids were playing, and the adults were working. I was helping my Grandma plant some flowers outside when all of a sudden everything darkened. The stars were shining as bright as they do at night. This was a solar eclipse. The way it looked was odd because I had never seen one. It was the Moon covering the Sun. The Sun was a big orange spot in the dark sky. It looked like a fire in the sky. It was so dark that the chickens went on their boards and the other animals went in the barn. When people went indoors, they had to turn on lanterns. After half an hour, the Moon began clearing from the Sun. People began to do their regular things and went on working, but afterwards everybody talked about it.

**CLAUDIA FLORES**
**PRESCOTT, ARIZONA**

---

*The Story—Part 3*     **25**

▶ continued from page 25

outside, she found the trunk of her Chevy Malibu totally demolished. Sitting in a shallow depression underneath the car was a 27-pound (12.3-kilogram) stony meteorite. It was still warm to the touch. The football-sized meteorite was apparently only a small piece of a much larger object. Before smacking into the student's car, the meteorite streaked across the evening sky. It was witnessed all along the eastern United States.

Similarly, in August 1972 visitors to Grand Teton National Park observed an extremely bright object cross the sky in broad daylight. The object was estimated to weigh upwards of several thousand tons. It narrowly missed striking Earth, grazing off the protective shield of our atmosphere back into space.

One outstanding meteorite strike can be found in Northern Arizona. Called the Barringer Crater, this meteorite scar is 3,900 feet wide and 600 feet deep. Scientists believe that a nickel-iron meteorite 200 feet across slammed into the Arizona desert 50,000 years ago. As much as 20 megatons of energy was released from the direct hit. There have been other cosmic impacts throughout Earth's geologic history. Aerial and satellite images have helped to find almost 200 craters around our planet.

On the surface, Earth appears to be a planet that has escaped the brutal bombardment so evident on other planets. Looks can be deceiving, however. The effects of weathering and erosion caused by rain, wind, freezing, and thawing have worked hard to remove the telltale signs of most impacts on Earth. In spite of that, more and more asteroid impact sites are being identified each year.

Sometimes, without our ever knowing it, Earth has near misses with asteroids and comets. Examples are becoming easy to find: in 1989 a half-mile-wide asteroid rushed past Earth at only twice the Moon's distance—480,000 miles. Had the asteroid come along 8 hours later, Earth would have just missed colliding with it.

In early 1991 a three-story-tall asteroid hurtled by Earth a mere 100,000 miles away. Similarly, in May 1993 an asteroid estimated to have a mass of 6,000 tons—about the weight of a naval destroyer—slipped by Earth just 90,000 miles away. This is the closest encounter with a wayward rock to date. This asteroid was detected only after it had passed by!

Some scientists now believe that a belt of small asteroids is in an orbit similar to that of Earth's. If true, we should expect more encounters with small (less than 50-meter-wide) chunks of space flotsam. They would not pose any hazard to Earth since they probably would not be able to survive a dive through Earth's atmosphere.

Beyond Earth, you do not have to look very far to assess the destructive nature of cosmic impacts. Earth's own Moon has clearly been the victim of a jarring rain of meteorite and asteroid collisions. Interplanetary probes dispatched from Earth have also relayed images of Mercury and its numerous craters. ■

# Great Balls of Fire

Satellites orbiting high above Earth have been spotting intense flashes of light in the Earth's atmosphere since the 1970's. Analysis of the data now suggests that Earth's atmosphere is invaded by comets and asteroids on a regular basis.

In October 1990, two military Defense Support Program (DSP) satellites recorded a burst of light over the western Pacific Ocean. Later analysis of the DSP data showed that the fireball that streaked across Earth's atmosphere released the energy equivalent to 500 tons of high explosives. That powerful a blast would have been caused by a 20,000-metric-ton meteor.

Between 1975 and 1992, satellites observed 136 flashes of light. Initial analysis indicates none of the objects reached the surface of Earth. But there are many more asteroids and comets out there that just might come too close for comfort. In 1992 it was reported that as many as fifty mini-asteroids may be passing between Earth and the Moon every day!

# Unanswered Questions About the Moon

1. What is the origin of the Moon?
2. Why are lunar rocks magnetic when the Moon has no magnetic field?
3. What is the chemical composition of the entire Moon?
4. Why is the Moon asymmetric, with volcanic lava (maria) concentrated on the Earth-facing side?
5. Does the Moon have a metal core?
6. How young are the youngest volcanic lavas on the Moon? How old are the oldest ones?
7. Is there frozen water in the permanently shadowed regions of the lunar poles?
8. Are there undiscovered types of lunar rock with unusual chemistries?
9. Are there geological processes on the Moon that concentrate important chemical elements such as useful metals?
10. What is the physical and chemical nature of the lunar regolith (soil)? What is the gas content?
11. What would be the best methods for extracting and fabricating useful materials from lunar rocks and soil?

# Theories of the Origin of the Moon

The origin of the Moon is a debatable subject. One theory—the *coformation* (or sister) theory—suggests that Earth and the Moon formed as planet and satellite at the same time about 4.5 billion years ago.

The *capture* theory maintains that the Moon formed far from Earth and orbited the Sun. Its planetary path passed close enough to be captured by Earth's gravity.

A third idea—the *fission* (or daughter) theory—speculates that the Moon was once a part of primordial Earth. Also called the escape theory, it contends that the Moon was formed from material that was torn away from Earth long ago at a time when the young Earth was rotating more rapidly than now. It also suggested the gravitational pull of the Sun on a mostly molten Earth could have caused a bulge on one side of Earth (perhaps where the Pacific Ocean basin is now) that broke away and moved out to its current orbit.

Today, many astronomers support a combination of the capture and fission theories, often labeled the *impact* theory. The hypothesis is that a large, Mars-sized object collided with a young and molten Earth.

Such collisions were a common occurrence in the earliest era of our solar system. Scientists postulate that this massive collision was more likely a glancing blow than a direct impact. The matter broke loose from Earth, then became the Moon.

The impact theory is supported by the fact that the composition of the Moon is similar to the material in Earth's mantle which lies between the crust and the core. This also helps explain the fact that the Moon lacks a dense central core.

*The north pole of the Moon*

# Moon Missions

When President John F. Kennedy said, "We choose to go to the Moon, not because it is easy, but because it is hard," he found eager, daring young people willing to undergo rigorous training for the opportunity to soar into space and walk on the Moon.

Through the centuries, the Moon has been an inspiration to poets, songwriters, and lovers. During the late sixties and early seventies, it became the target of six Apollo missions from Earth. On July 20, 1969, *Apollo 11* made the first landing on the Moon. The sixth and last Apollo exploration mission occurred in December 1972.

Lack of atmosphere on the Moon insures that the *regolith*—the Moon's dusty surface—will remain forever imprinted with American astronauts' adventurous footsteps.

However, the astronauts did not claim the Moon for the United States. In 1967 more than 90 nations signed a space exploration treaty that declares the Moon and outer space to be off limits to such claims of ownership. The space exploration treaty also prohibits the use of space for military purposes.

*Far side of the Moon, photographed during the* Apollo 16 *mission*

---

**STUDENT VOICES**

Last night there was a lunar eclipse. It was like a bite out of the Moon that kept getting bigger and bigger until the whole Moon was hidden from view. Then it started coming into view on the other side. Lunar eclipses helped prove the world was round (the shadow cast by the Earth had a kind of depth to it that only a sphere could cast). It was really neat to watch, especially since I understood why it was happening. This was the first celestial event I had ever seen; now I'm intrigued.

EMILY GRIFFIN
PRESCOTT, ARIZONA

# Planetary Scientist

**DR. DAVID MORRISON**
**NASA AMES RESEARCH**
**CENTER**
**MOFFETT FIELD, CALIFORNIA**

You could say I'm in the asteroid business. I am the chief of the Space Science Division here at the National Aeronautics and Space Administration's (NASA's) Ames Research Center near San Francisco, California. I have a wide range of responsibilities here at NASA. They include astrophysics, planetary science, and *exobiology* (that's the study of life beyond Earth).

As a planetary scientist, I recently chaired an important group of 24 scientists and engineers. Our team took part in the International Near Earth Object Detection Workshop.

One of our duties was to investigate how potentially hazardous asteroids could be detected much more rapidly. When we completed our work, we made a number of recommendations to our fellow NASA workers, as well as to Congress and to the public through the media. I keep waiting for NASA to start giving me awards. I've been working on asteroids for several years now, and we haven't been hit yet.

One of my concerns is how the public might have difficulties understanding the statistical estimates of human risk and the hazard of an asteroid striking Earth. The impact threat is real, and it is of a magnitude at least as great as many other natural disasters such as tornadoes, earthquakes, floods, and hurricanes.

We should take both asteroid and comet impacts seriously, but, to be honest, I worry more about comets smacking into Earth than I do asteroids. Comets are very difficult to accurately track; they can change course very unexpectedly. Unlike other natural disasters, comet and asteroid impacts can be avoided. We have the ability to protect our planet if we choose to do so.

Unfortunately, only a very small fraction of the public has heard of asteroids or comets impacting Earth. In July 1994 there was an unprecedented astronomical event. In fact, you could call it a "wake-up call" for everyone here on Earth. Pieces of a large comet slammed into Jupiter. It could have been us being jolted. It has happened before and will happen again.

My primary interests are in astronomy and planetary science, with a special focus on the smaller bodies in the solar system such as asteroids, comets, and moons around other planets. My NASA job is really the product of my interest in science and astronomy I've had since I was very young. Some people say that a lot of kids are interested in astronomy, but most of them outgrow it. I didn't!

I really had no idea of what kind of astronomy I wanted to do until I reached graduate school, believe it or not. In my first year there, I took a course on the planets from astronomer Carl Sagan. That convinced me I wanted to do planetary astronomy. Until then, I probably shared the bias of most astro-nomers that planets were not a very interesting subject for research.

I feel very fortunate to have participated as a scientist in the *Mariner 10* mission to Venus and then Mercury, as well as the Voyager planetary missions to Jupiter, Saturn, Uranus, and Neptune. And, by the way, I'm honored to have my own, personalized heavenly body. Asteroid 2410 Morrison is named after me!

IN THE NEWS

By Matt Mendelsohn, USA TODAY
**GOING, GOING, GONE:** Earth's shadow eclipses the moon.

**LUNAR ECLIPSE:** Parts of the USA saw an early evening lunar eclipse Wednesday, but other areas weren't as lucky, as clouds and sunshine prevented viewing. It lasted about three hours. Traditionally called the "blood of the moon" because the moon usually looks red, this eclipse was hazy gray, Kevin Roth of Weather Service Corp. said. Such a moon has been thought to portend the fall of Chinese dynasties.

USA TODAY, DECEMBER 10, 1992

# Working as a Team of Two— Philip and Phylis Morrison

Although there can be many influences on your career choice—experiences, friends, heroes, teachers, family—most people enter into the work force on their own. For some people, however, the person they decide to marry ends up becoming their business partner as well.

Such is the case for Philip and Phylis Morrison. They have worked as a team for years on numerous projects—television specials and series, books, articles, and science teacher workshops. One of their famous productions, in both book and video form, is called *The Powers of Ten.* It takes the viewer from inside the atom to outside of our galaxy by magnitudes of ten. Also take a look at the book and video of their Public Broadcasting Service (PBS) series called *The Ring of Truth: An Inquiry Into How We Know What We Know.*

Phylis has taught science and art at all levels from kindergarten through university. She and Philip have worked together for decades creating exciting ways to help teachers and students, as well as the public, understand science.

Here is how they tackle a task. In some cases, after deciding on the various aspects of a project, they work separately on different segments of the task, then sit down together, edit each

*Phyllis and Philip Morrison hold a photograph of an astrolabe.*

other's work, and smooth over the final product. For other ventures, they work closely together throughout the project.

As you work with your team on the task for this unit, decide which activities are best suited to work on together, and which are better accomplished by one member or a team of two.

Here is some additional advice from Phylis Morrison: "Add a little humor to your project. The possibility of an asteroid impact with Earth is a genuinely scary subject. There

can be a lighter road. Don't overdo it, but try using a certain amount of playfulness, make-believe, or even science fiction. When you don't have a lot of facts at your fingertips, you can start with the facts you do have and embellish them. Think about the contributions Mark Twain might make if he were a member of your team."(Note: Mark Twain was born in 1835 when Halley's Comet passed close to Earth. He died 76 years later with the return of the comet in 1910.)

# Origin and Fate of the Universe

One of the most commonly known explanations of the origin of the universe is the Big Bang Theory, also referred to as the expanding universe or evolutionary theory. It states that about 14.5 billion years ago, all matter and radiation was concentrated in a dense, glowing mass. Then that concentrated point exploded and billions of galaxies flew apart at high speeds, moving away from each other in all directions.

Beyond the Big Bang Theory, several models attempt to explain the fate of the universe: the open universe, the closed universe, and the critical universe.

The *open universe* model contends that when the explosion occurred, there was not enough matter for gravity to stop the expansion, so the universe will never return to the state it was in before the Big Bang.

If the density of matter thrown out by the Big Bang is greater than the "critical value"—dense enough to cause the universe to stop expanding—then the *closed universe* model would be correct. The Big Bang would reverse, and all the matter in the universe would collapse onto itself.

A third explanation, the *critical universe* model, suggests that the density of the universe is exactly equal to the "critical value." This would mean that the accumulated matter is just sufficient to eventually halt the expansion, but only after an infinitely long time. If correct, the critical universe would not have occurred by chance; it would be a consequence of the laws of physics.

An alternative theory to the Big Bang was developed in the 1940s and 1950s and still has a few supporters. It is the model of the *steady-state universe*. It maintains that the universe appears the same to all observers, and that it has appeared the same throughout all time. The universe has no beginning and no end. Most astronomers see this theory as fatally flawed, because it defies some of the laws of physics.

The NASA Hubble Space Telescope now orbiting Earth and the Cosmic Background Explorer Satellite (COBE) are two of the many tools astronomers use to study the universe. These devices and other astronomical satellites, as well as ground-based observatories, provide a continual flow of new information about our universe.

Though knowledge of our celestial neighborhood has vastly increased, especially in the last few decades, many questions still remain unanswered. These unsolved mysteries await the curious minds of young people such as you and your classmates.

## Satellite gives boost to 'Big Bang' theory

Scientists using NASA's Cosmic Background Explorer satellite to measure thermal radiation differences across the universe said Thursday they have the best evidence yet to support the "Big Bang" theory that the universe was created by a single blast 15 billion years ago. The "afterglow" of the Big Bang showed 99.97% of the universe's radiant energy was released within the first year. "This is the ultimate in tracing one's cosmic roots," said NASA's John Mather at the American Astronomical Society meeting in Phoenix.

**A star is born**

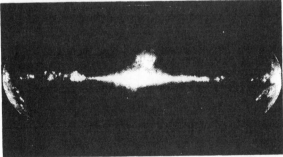

NASA via AP

**WHERE STARS COME FROM:** NASA's Cosmic Background Explorer satellite photographed dusty regions of the Milky Way, which are our galaxy's 'stellar nurseries.'

USA TODAY, JANUARY 8, 1993

# Venus—Hothouse of the Heavens

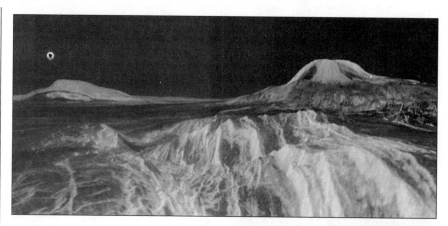

Venus is often called the "morning star" or "evening star." When it's visible, it is one of the brightest objects in the sky. Venus can be seen just before sunrise or just after sunset. It appears more than ten times brighter than Sirius, the brightest star visible from Earth. In fact, Venus is the third brightest object in the entire sky, after the Sun and Moon.

Viewing Venus from Earth, we see that our closest planet neighbor has phases similar to our Moon's phases. Venus actually appears brightest in its crescent phase because it is closer to us than when it is full. Sometimes you can even see Venus during the day, if you know where to look.

Although it is similar to Earth in both size and density, the surface pressure on Venus is 90 times the surface pressure on Earth. Venus is shrouded in clouds consisting primarily of sulfuric acid droplets, and its atmosphere consists mainly of carbon dioxide.

Visible light from the Sun passes through the Venusian atmosphere only to be absorbed by the surface and changed into infrared radiation. Largely because of the carbon dioxide-laden atmosphere, the infrared rays cannot escape. The temperature of the atmosphere climbs to 500 degrees Celsius (C) or 900 degrees Fahrenheit (F). This phenomenon is known as the *greenhouse effect*.

If the atmosphere of Earth did not trap some of the heat in a similar manner, our average surface temperature would be much colder. However, if the atmosphere on Earth became unbalanced—for example, by having large quantities of carbon dioxide discharged into it—a runaway greenhouse effect could happen on Earth.

Impact craters, extinct faults, and dormant volcanoes of Venus were revealed by the *Magellan* spacecraft. Its radar "eyes" saw through the cloud cover and mapped 95 percent of the surface of the planet by 1992.

Since Venus was named for

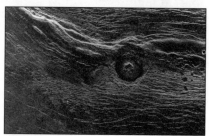

**The northern part of the Akna Montes (mountains) of Venus**

the Roman goddess of love and beauty and since many new features were found by *Magellan*, the National Aeronautics and Space Administration (NASA) began taking suggestions from the public of famous women's names for these features.

# NASA find out of this . . . system

By Paul Hoversten
USA TODAY

Far-flung Pluto is far from the edge of our solar system. NASA said Wednesday radio waves are the first direct evidence of the heliopause, the line between the solar system and interstellar space.

Voyagers 1 and 2 detected the waves, caused by solar and interstellar particles colliding, at a distance that more than doubles the popular view of our system's size.

The boundary seems to fall between 8.3 billion and 11.1 billion miles from the sun:

▶ Earth is 93 million miles from the sun.
▶ Pluto, 3.6 billion miles.

NASA
**VENUS:** Simulated-color photo shows global view of planet, Earth's neighbor

"This is an incredible victory" for the 15-year-old spacecraft, says Mary Hardin at NASA's Jet Propulsion Laboratory, Pasadena, Calif.

Both Voyagers are already past Pluto, but it could take either 20 years — traveling at 279 million miles a year — to hit the start of the boundary.

"You can't eat it or sell it or peddle it," says University of Chicago physicist Eugene Parker of the heliopause. "One would just sort of like to know what's out there."

Elsewhere in the solar system, NASA's Magellan probe — which mapped nearly all of Venus' volcanic surface — is moving into the cloudy atmosphere to study its gravity.

During the next 80 days, Magellan will use Venus' atmospheric drag to reshape its course, the first use of a technique called "aerobraking."

USA TODAY, MAY 27, 1993

# Impact Craters

Evidence of asteroid or comet impacts is not as apparent on Earth as it is on other planets and moons. Erosion over the centuries, especially from running water and wind, has weathered away or buried many craters. In addition, since 70 percent of Earth's surface is water, impact craters beneath the surface are especially hard to find.

Using satellite photography, nearly 100 craters larger than a tenth of a kilometer (328 feet) in diameter have been identified.

The most visible meteorite crater in the United States is near Winslow, Arizona, and measures almost 1.2 kilometers (4,000 feet) across. Geologists estimate that the responsible meteorite hit Earth about 50,000 years ago.

Another impact crater is centered on the coast of the Yucatan Peninsula in the Gulf of Mexico. Some geophysicists link this evidence of an asteroid hit to the extinction of the dinosaurs. It was recently discovered that the crater is larger than originally estimated. It measures 300 kilometers (190 miles) in diameter and is thought to be 65 million years old.

# Earth—The Luckiest Planet

Earth is fifth in size among the planets and third in distance from the Sun. Its incredible uniqueness and beauty staggers the mind. Earth has temperatures without intolerable extremes and a surface that is 70 percent water and 30 percent land. It has all of the oxygen and water needed to sustain life as we know it. No other planet in our solar system has these necessities in exactly the right proportions. In fact, on Earth we have the perfect site for the evolution of an abundant and diverse array of life forms.

Twenty-four hours marks one rotation of Earth on its tilted axis. It is that tilt in relationship to the Sun that causes the seasons. Like a toy top winding down, the Earth spins and slightly wobbles as it travels its orbit around the Sun. This consistent wobble is produced by the gravitational pull of the Moon.

| Known Impact Craters on Earth | | |
|---|---|---|
| Location | Diam. (km) | Age (millions of years) |
| Russia | 10 | 4.5 |
| Russia | 10 | 10.0 |
| Ghana | 11 | 1.0 |
| Libya | 12 | 120.0 |
| Canada | 12 | 100.0 |
| Brazil | 12 | 300.0 |
| Canada | 13 | 450.0 |
| USA, Texas | 13 | 100.0 |
| USA, Indiana | 13 | 300.0 |
| Finland | 14 | 77.0 |
| USA, Tenn. | 14 | 200.0 |
| Russia | 14 | 700.0 |
| Russia | 15 | 160.0 |
| Sweden | 15 | 230.0 |
| Russia | 15 | 360.0 |
| Russia | 17 | 100.0 |
| Russia | 19 | 3.4 |
| Canada | 20 | 15.0 |
| Australia | 22 | 130.0 |
| Canada | 22 | 290.0 |
| France | 23 | 160.0 |
| Canada | 23 | 225.0 |
| Germany | 24 | 15.0 |
| Australia | 24 | 600.0 |
| Canada | 25 | 95.0 |
| Russia | 26 | 65.0 |
| Canada | 28 | 38.0 |
| Australia | 28 | 1,690.0 |
| Canada | 30 | 350.0 |
| USA, Iowa | 32 | 70.0 |
| Canada | 32 | 290.0 |
| Canada | 37 | 485.0 |
| Brazil | 40 | 250.0 |
| Canada | 46 | 360.0 |
| Russia | 50 | 57.0 |
| Sweden | 52 | 365.0 |
| Canada | 70 | 210.0 |
| Russia | 80 | 183.0 |
| Russia | 100 | 39.0 |
| Canada | 140 | 1,840.0 |
| S. Africa | 140 | 1,970.0 |
| Mexico | 300 | 65.0 |

# Mars—The Red Planet

Mars is little more than half the size of Earth. Mars has unusual surface features, including huge extinct volcanoes and massive canyons. The largest volcano, Olympus Mons, rises into the Martian sky nearly three times the height of Mount Everest, the tallest mountain on Earth.

Valles Marineris is much larger than our Grand Canyon. It cuts across the terrain of Mars and spans 4,800 kilometers (3,000 miles), the distance between New York and Los Angeles.

Mars, like Earth, is tilted on its axis. Astronomers have observed that its polar ice caps melt in the summer and freeze in the winter. These ice caps may be (as some data suggest) the only source of water on the planet unless water is frozen underground in what is called the *permafrost.*

Mars, which was named for the Roman god of war, has two moons; the larger moon is Phobos and the smaller is Deimos. Their names in Greek mean "fear" and "terror"— appropriate attendants for a warlike god. A case can be made for the theory that Phobos and Deimos were asteroids taken hostage long ago by the gravity of Mars.

Although it lacks a magnetic field of its own, Mars is a magnet for planetary scientists and space enthusiasts who advocate sending humans to explore our nearest inhabitable planet.

In the mid-1970s, NASA sent the *Viking I* and *II* robot landers to the Martian surface. The spacecraft sent back amazing images of the planet's reddish, rocky terrain.

Scientific instruments on the *Viking* landers also looked for signs of life on Mars. The instruments detected no evidence of organic compounds in the soil within the range of sensitivity of the instruments. However, some planetary scientists contend that the experiments did not ask the

*Mosaic of the Valles Marineris hemisphere of Mars*

*The Martian landscape photographed by the* Viking 1 *lander, showing a dune field with features similar to many seen in deserts on Earth*

right questions. The results are puzzling and still controversial today.

Liquid water once flowed on the surface of Mars, leaving behind dry riverbeds. Exobiologists (biologists who study the possibility of life on other celestial bodies) are especially interested in exploring the dry riverbeds, the deep canyons, and the polar caps. Since life as we know it needs water to survive, exobiologists believe that these regions might harbor evidence of past or present microscopic life.

Future international missions to Mars include plans to drop scientific instruments into the Martian atmosphere. The instruments will be attached to a balloon that will float above the surface.

Robotics experts and university students are designing small automated rovers that could be launched to Mars by the end of the century. The rovers would roam the surface collecting soil samples that would be rocketed back to Earth for detailed analysis.

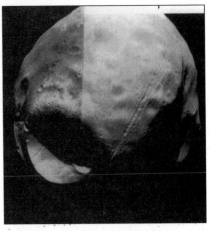

*Mars' moon Phobes, photographed at a range of 380 miles by* **Viking Orbiter 1**

**SCIENCE ACTIVITY**

# Solar System Business Guide

## Purpose
To invent two fictional businesses that are suited for one location in the solar system; design a newspaper and/or magazine advertisement for the businesses. The ads should include a description of location. You should also create a "Solar System Business Guide."

## Materials
- Astronomy resource books (this module and others)
- Construction paper
- Markers
- Discovery File "Charting the Planets" (page 20)

## Activity
Background: Your advertising agency's contract with the AAEC includes designing a campaign to better familiarize the public with the solar system. You and your staff have decided to use print media (newspapers and magazines) for advertisements about fictional businesses located in different parts of the solar system. You think these will attract attention better than purely informational pieces.

1. You will be assigned one location in the solar system. Research the characteristics of that location and develop two imaginary businesses that suit the location's characteristics. For example, if the Sun is your location, you might think it would be a great place for a high-speed bakery or a high-volume nuclear waste incinerator.

2. Develop one advertisement for each of your fictional businesses. For each advertisement, do the following:
   - Make a diagram or drawing of the assigned location.
   - Identify special characteristics (such as size, gravity, atmosphere, lengths of days and years, and so on) with tables or other graphics to illustrate the facts.
   - Describe the name and function of the business you develop.
   - Think of fictitious prices for services and/or products.

3. When you teacher directs you to, post your completed ads in the classroom. View other students' ads and take notes on the information about the location in the solar system you get by looking at the ads.

4. With your team, compile notes on the ads into a solar system information chart. The chart could look similar to the one in the Discovery File "Charting the Planets" on page 20.

5. With your team, use the solar system information chart and the descriptions of the fictitious businesses to create a "Solar System Business Guide."

# Comet a jolt to Jupiter

By Paul Hoversten
USA TODAY

Jupiter is due for a cosmic collision like the one believed to have wiped out dinosaurs 65 million years ago.

Comet Shoemaker-Levy 9 — now orbiting Jupiter — is due to plunge into the planet's gaseous atmosphere around July 23, 1994.

"This could be a real live example of the phenomenon that may have killed the dinosaurs," says Steve Maran, American Astronomical Society. "An astronomer has to be happy he's alive."

NASA's Hubble Space Telescope looks at the comet next week. But the collision is expected to happen on Jupiter's far side — out of view.

Last year, the comet came so close that Jupiter's enormous gravity tore it into about 20 pieces with the largest about 3 miles across.

The pieces are expected to hit Jupiter's atmosphere at up to 36 miles a second, each releasing the equivalent of 1 billion megatons of TNT, some scientists say.

Largest nuclear explosion on Earth: 60 megatons.

But with Jupiter 11 times bigger than Earth, the impact might be "like throwing a stone into the ocean," says Dan Green, Central Bureau for Astronomical Telegrams.

Co-discoverer David Levy of Tucson, Ariz., says it just shows the universe's evolving nature. "It's like there's an 'Under Construction' sign out, with things happening right before our eyes."

USA TODAY, 25 JUNE, 1993

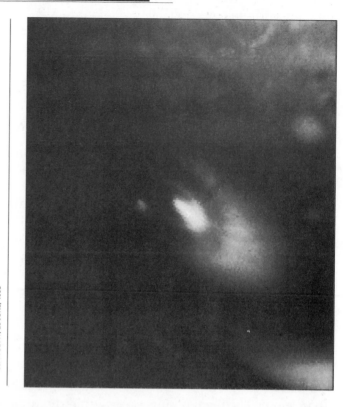

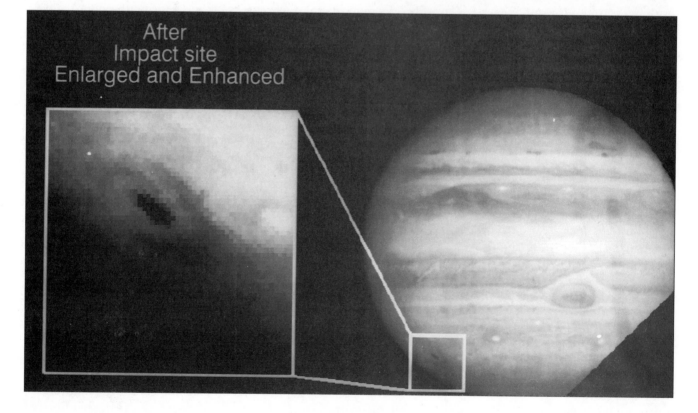

After
Impact site
Enlarged and Enhanced

# Jupiter—The Battle of the Bands

Jupiter, named for the chief god of the Romans, could swallow any one of the other planets in its turbulent mass. The gaseous giant is dwarfed only by the Sun, which is 1,000 times more massive.

Three outstanding features of Jupiter involve its atmosphere and its rotation. Its Great Red Spot is the site of a perpetual hurricane-like disturbance of gigantic proportions. Its speedy rotation gives it the shortest day—a mere 9 hours and 55 minutes. Its distinctive cloud bands, which display an array of colors, are believed to result from chemical compounds in its atmosphere.

Jupiter's axis is almost perpendicular to its orbital plane—with a tilt of 3 degrees compared to the 23.5-degree tilt of Earth. Since the tilt determines seasonal changes, Jupiter does not undergo major changes during the course of its 12-Earth-year orbit of the Sun.

With 16 moons, Jupiter is, in many ways, like a smaller version of our solar system. Its four largest satellites are similar in size to Earth's moon and are named for the attendants to Jove in classical mythology: Io, Europa, Ganymede, Callisto.

Io has acquired the nickname "pizza moon." As the most geologically active body in our solar system, Io's surface is continually being recreated by the intense volcanic activity that covers evidence of past impacts.

The surface of the Jovian moon Europa is the smoothest

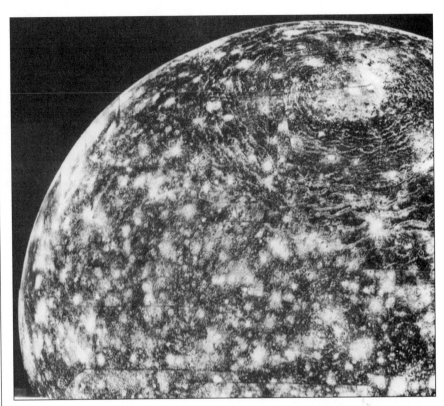

*This photomosaic of Jupiter's moon Calisto was assembled from pictures taken by* Voyager 1 *on March 6, 1979.*

in the solar system. With no mountains higher than 100 meters, some call it a "cosmic cue ball."

Ganymede is the largest moon in the solar system. Callisto, composed mostly of ice, bears the title of most cratered.

Voyager 1 *took this photograph of Jupiter on February 1, 1979.*

# A Crash Course in Comet Watching

The comet was first spotted on March 24, 1993, by Carolyn Shoemaker as she studied photographic plates of the heavens. From the start, she could tell that there was something strange about the object caught on camera.

Shoemaker, along with her space-geologist husband Eugene Shoemaker and amateur astronomer David Levy, typically spend long hours at the observatory atop Mount Palomar near San Diego, California. They are a special breed of sky-watchers, dedicated to scanning space for comets and asteroids.

On that March night, their celestial sleuthing paid off. They found a "new" comet. It was the ninth such object the Shoemaker-Levy team had detected that year, and as its discoverers they could name their catch of the night. The threesome called it Comet Shoemaker-Levy 9.

The first image taken of Comet Shoemaker-Levy 9 appeared squashed. Later pictures showed that the comet had actually split into a number of fragments. Pulled by the immense gravity grip of Jupiter, the comet had broken into about 20 pieces. It was no longer a single mountain of rock and ice, but a stretched-out chain of fragments. One astronomer saw them as a "string of pearls."

More observations of the comet were called for. Apparently, the object had been in orbit around Jupiter for a couple of decades or more. But in July 1992 it had passed so close to the planet, it lost a gravitational tug of war and ripped apart. Scientists were able to calculate its path, deducing that the comet was on a crash course with Jupiter.

For the first time in human history, astronomers had advance warning of the collision between two celestial objects. But what would happen in this astronomical version of fatal attraction? Some of the icy pieces were 2 miles across. From July 16 to July 22, 1994, Jupiter was going to be barraged by comet hits. Screaming into Jupiter at 134,000 miles per hour, the fate of the great comet chunks was anybody's guess.

On July 16, scientists around the globe watched Jupiter. At the Space Telescope Science Institute in Baltimore, Maryland, an auditorium of reporters gathered to hear first word about the great comet crash of 1994. Orbiting above Earth, the Hubble space telescope was focused on the planet. On the ground, observatories around the planet were on alert.

Unfortunately, the comet hits would take place on the back side of Jupiter as observed from Earth. Cautious astronomers had told the public that little in the way of impact effects was likely to be visible because Jupiter was so big. When the first comet fragment plowed into Jupiter, a huge plume of gas shot hundreds of miles above Jupiter's cloud tops. An explosion possibly equal to a million hydrogen bombs created a mushroom-like cloud. The cloud rose high enough and close enough to the edge of the planet to be observed by the Hubble Space telescope as well as ground-based telescopes. Scientists were elated. As Jupiter rotated into full view of Earth, a dark blemish about half the size of Earth could be seen in Jupiter's atmosphere.

"I'm just thrilled to pieces," remarked comet codiscoverer David Levy. Astronomer Heidi Hammel added, "This was in my dreams, what we saw." Hammel headed the team of Hubble Space Telescope scientists studying the effects on Jupiter of the comet bombardment. "It's going to be a great week," she said.

One by one, the giant comet fragments swooped into Jupiter's thick, swirling atmosphere. The planetary fireworks that were observed were beyond anybody's speculation. In total, 21 known comet pieces of Comet Shoemaker-Levy 9 struck Jupiter over 6 days. The colossal impacts rocked the planet with an energy force 500 times greater than all the nuclear bombs on Earth. Numbers of the dark scars could be seen at one time spread across the planet's face.

For Eugene Shoemaker, the Jupiter-comet crash was an astounding event. "It's the realization of a dream, of a fantasy, if you will," said Shoemaker. "I always dreamed that I might someday witness the impact of an asteroid or a comet . . . never really expecting that I would because the odds were just too small."

While the high velocity hits took place 400 million miles away on distant Jupiter, a similar event likely wiped out the dinosaurs on Earth 65 million years ago. Is the comet collision with Jupiter yet another wake-up call for Earth to be on guard? How should Earth's population view the great comet crash? "They're lucky they don't live on Jupiter," responded one astronomer. Indeed, if Shoemaker-Levy 9 had hit Earth, the results would have been catastrophic. "We should stay alert to watch for comets and Earth-crossing asteroids. I think that's very worthwhile, but the odds that we're going to get hit with a really damaging impact are very low in our lifetime," Eugene Shoemaker explained. However, there is no telling what surprises for Earth are lurking out there in the depths of space. ■

*A NASA image of comet P/Shoemaker-Levy 9, taken May 17, 1994, showing the comet's train of 21 icy fragments*

*These four images of Jupiter and the impact of fragment W of Shoemaker-Levy 9 were taken by the Galileo spacecraft, July 22, 1994. The first image shows no impact, but in the next three images, a point of light appears on Jupiter's night side, brightens, then fades.*

# Jupiter hit with a 'big wallop'

## Spectacular strike due Wednesday

By Paul Hoversten
USA TODAY

GREENBELT, Md. — The biggest chunks yet of a comet pounded Jupiter's atmosphere Monday with an explosive force almost beyond comprehension, leaving black smears larger than Earth.

"It's a big wallop," says comet co-discoverer Eugene Shoemaker, reporting that a fragment called G flared as bright as Jupiter itself on heat-measuring telescopes.

At the South African Astronomical Observatory's Sutherland station, astronomers saw "a gigantic fireball, much bigger than anything we have seen" from the next piece, called H, says Doug Whittet of the Rensselaer Polytechnic Institute, Troy, N.Y.

"This holds out much promise for a truly spectacular detonation Wednesday when the largest piece of the comet hits," says Whittet.

All 21 of the comet pieces will hit Jupiter's backside, out of direct Earth view.

The impacts are leaving huge black blotches in Jupiter's upper atmosphere that expand rapidly through the clouds in the southern latitudes.

"At this rate, Jupiter will look like it's got a bad case of measles by the time the last fragments hit," says Bob Stobie, director of the South African station, about 225 miles northwest of Cape Town.

Scientists are star struck over the comet bombardment as mysterious effects, telescope limitations and even bad weather hamper observations.

"None of this stuff is anything we had expected to see," says Heidi Hammel, Massachusetts Institute of Technology. "We're moving well into the realm of speculation."

Fragment G, estimated at 2½ miles across, hit with 25 times the force of the first piece, which hit Saturday.

Fragment G may have plunged 36 miles into Jupiter's atmosphere before collapsing on itself and erupting in a superheated gas bubble that rose 1,300 miles above the planet.

"The energy released is beyond any of our experiences on Earth," says astronomer Lucy McFadden, of the University of Maryland.

Had the fragment struck Earth, it would have left a crater 37 miles wide and sent dust and debris into the atmosphere, says Shoemaker.

But it wasn't comparable to the asteroid that carved a 111-mile crater in the Yucatan 65 million years ago and is believed linked to the demise of the dinosaurs. "This is a big event, but it still isn't the dinosaur killer," says Shoemaker.

So bright were the infrared flashes of the biggest comet fragments that telescope detectors at the W.M. Keck Observatory atop Mauna Kea, Hawaii, became "saturated" with photons, preventing astronomers from recording the amount of light.

"It's like having a (video) camcorder in a dark room and then somebody throws open a door and everything on the film goes white," says John Clarke, a space physicist at the University of Michigan.

The comet fragments are leaving Earth-sized dark splotches on Jupiter's gaseous atmosphere where the pieces flew in at 37 miles per second. Jupiter's diameter is about 11 times that of the Earth.

How the comet material spreads out over time may help scientists determine the wind speed and direction of Jupiter's upper atmosphere.

The heat of the supercharged impacts appears to be producing new molecules or ions. These show up as strange "emission lines" in the upper atmosphere.

"We're dealing with big objects here and there are some big ones yet to come," says Shoemaker.

Jupiter should come through the barrage without too much permanent damage. "I think Jupiter's going to hang in there," says Hammel. "We're seeing these black eyes, big splotches and bruises and I almost feel sorry for Jupiter."

*Contributing: Chris Erasmus in South Africa*

## Big chunk hits Jupiter

The biggest of the first seven fragments of the Comet Shoemaker-Levy 9 slammed into Jupiter Monday with an energy 75 times the force of the Earth's nuclear arsenal.

**1** 2.5-mile diameter comet fragment on crash-course for Jupiter's dark side.

**2** Fragment punches 36 miles into Jupiter's atmosphere, forming a fireball. The infrared light is as bright as the whole planet of Jupiter normally appears, and briefly blinds some observing instruments on Earth.

**3** Hot gas bubble rises 1,367 miles over Jupiter's surface – so high observers on Earth can see it protruding over Jupiter's horizon. Bubble spreads out in a black smear.

**4** Earlier impacts left black pockmarks in a band on the southern end of Jupiter. Marks spreading out and some now are bigger in diameter than Earth.

### Comet comparisons
A look at the magnitude of the impact:

**Explosive force (in megatons of TNT)**

| | |
|---|---|
| Comet | 6 million |
| Earth's nuclear arsenal | 80,000 |

**Speed**

| | |
|---|---|
| Comet as it hit Jupiter | 134,000 mph |
| Space shuttle in Earth orbit | 17,500 mph |

**Temperature (Degrees Fahrenheit)**

| | |
|---|---|
| Comet impact | 53,550 |
| Surface of sun | 10,350 |

Sources: NASA, *The Nuclear Almanac*, The AP

By Stephen Conley, USA TODAY

USA TODAY, JULY 19, 1994

# Impacts prove a puzzlement

By Tim Friend
USA TODAY

GREENBELT, Md.— Comet Shoemaker-Levy 9 is blasting holes in scientists' expectations, leaving them to ponder new mysteries about Jupiter.

The latest: an Earth-sized "black eye" and the dark bruise-like spots created by the astronomical assault.

"The impacts have behaved contrary to our assumptions," says Keith Noll, astronomer at the Space Telescope Science Institute, Baltimore.

The dark marks, made by fireballs after pieces hit, are a mix of chemicals and particles in the upper atmosphere. Their exact composition is unknown.

Astronomer Lucy McFadden of the University of Maryland says scientists are puzzled that images taken with special filters have found no chemical signature for water.

Some scientists had speculated that the comet was composed partly of ice and would deliver water into the Jovian atmosphere.

Scientists also expected comet fragments to churn up water clouds that exist in the planet's atmosphere just below a layer of ammonia, McFadden says.

"Instead of bright white clouds in the visible spectrum due to water vapor, we get the opposite effect," says Noll.

Scientists have been able to answer some questions about the dark spots' composition by using telescopes that work in the realm of invisible light, detecting chemicals visible only in the infrared or ultraviolet light spectrums.

The studies should reveal a range of reactions in Jupiter's atmosphere. So far, measurements of impact sites reveal ammonia that was not there before, says Noll. The uppermost clouds of Jupiter are made of ammonia ice crystals.

"We see a large increase in the amount of ammonia," says Noll. "And one simple way to get that is to get a large release of energy, dissolve the ammonia and release it as gas."

The chemical composition of the sites also should yield information about how far the comet fragments penetrate Jupiter's atmosphere.

While water apparently was not churned up from below the visible clouds, "there are hints in our data of other gases that indicate the fragments may have gone deeper," says Noll.

Scientists also were puzzling over how the features of a great black eye were formed.

McFadden likens the ring to the pattern made in a swimming pool when a diver does a "can opener." The horseshoe shape may have formed because the comet fragments are bombarding Jupiter from a 45-degree angle.

▶ **Black eye, 1A**

USA TODAY, 20 JULY, 1994

# Comet's punch leaves 'black eye' on Jupiter

By Tim Friend
USA TODAY

GREENBELT, Md. — Jupiter now has a "black eye" to match its Great Red Spot.

The largest fragment so far of Comet Shoemaker-Levy 9 left "the most visually prominent discrete spot in 384 years of observing Jupiter," says Steve Maran of the Goddard Space Flight Center.

NASA photos released Tuesday reveal an Earth-sized dark spot and a larger horseshoe ring caused by the impact of fragment G, which hit Monday.

The planet has been studied since 1610 with early telescopes. The Great Red Spot is an atmospheric storm that's been observed for centuries.

About fragments H and K:
▶ Maran says one observatory reported H created a blast

| Result of impact causes a puzzle, **3A** |
| --- |

50 times brighter than Jupiter.
▶ Fragment K created a fireball with an afterglow about three times Earth's size.

The fireworks are dazzling, but astronomers are baffled by the fragments' effects on Jupiter's atmosphere.

They expected the impacts to create bright white clouds containing water. Instead, the comet chunks have dotted Jupiter's southern region with mysterious black marks, says Keith Noll, Space Telescope Science Institute in Baltimore.

"We don't know what to make of seeing no water," says Noll, who adds that studies of the composition of the dark spots are under way.

Still to come: a "triple whammy" of three comet chunks beginning today, each striking Jupiter in roughly the same spot 10 hours apart.

Under the best viewing conditions — no clouds, no outdoor light — amateurs with 8-inch or larger telescopes now may be able to spot the spots.

USA TODAY, JULY 20, 1994

# Mine Your Own Business

Instead of taking a duck-and-cover approach toward asteroids passing near Earth, why not think of them as potential treasure chests of exotic minerals? Asteroids are subdivided into categories based on spectroscopic evidence: how much light of different color is reflected by an asteroid. Some asteroids carry water locked up in them. Certain classes of asteroids contain alloys of iron, nickel, and cobalt. Other asteroids appear to carry such valuable resources as titanium and manganese.

The prospects of mining these valuable minerals once caught the attention of then Vice President Lyndon Johnson. As he opened up the 1962 Seattle World's Fair, he said, "Someday we will be able to bring an asteroid containing billions of dollars worth of critically needed metals close to Earth to provide a vast source of mineral wealth to our factories."

Mining engineers are eyeing Earth-crossing asteroids with just that thought in mind. According to one recent estimate, an asteroid of only 1 kilometer in diameter would have a mass of about 2 billion tons. Of that total, about 200 million tons would be metals.

How would you set up a mining operation on an asteroid?

# Orbit Logo

## Purpose
To draw a scale model of the inner planets with their orbits, to draw the orbit of an asteroid approaching the inner planets, and to calculate orbit eccentricity.

## Materials
- Large piece of paper (at least 60 cm × 100 cm)
- 2 straight pins
- 3 meters of string
- Pencil
- Cardboard (at least the size of your paper, you may have to tape together several pieces)
- Meter stick
- Scissors
- Compass

## Activity
Background: Your advertising agency has decided to design and illustrate a scale drawing of the inner planets showing the path of an approaching asteroid. The Graphic Arts Department has developed a laboratory activity that they think is suitable for middle school students. You have been asked to:
- Test the instructions to see if they can be followed by middle school students.
- Add details to the drawing to make it factually correct and visually appealing.

The Graphic Arts Department also plans to use the orbit drawing for an AAEC logo. You will make a scale drawing that shows orbits of the inner planets and the orbit of an approaching asteroid. After you have completed the three parts of the procedure, add details and graphics to make the final product eye-catching.

## Part One—Draw Orbits
1. Place the paper on top of the cardboard so the long dimension runs from left to right. From the top left corner, measure down half of the width of the paper, then measure to the right 20 cm. Mark this point with a dot, push a pin through the dot into the cardboard, and label it "Sun." Do not move this pin during the rest of the experiment.
2. Refer to the data table. Position the second pin the correct distance to the right of the Sun to represent the next planet. Note: The pins do not represent the planets—they are only place holders to help you draw the planets' orbits.
3. Cut a piece of string a little bit longer than the distance given in the chart for that planet's orbit loop. Tie the string into a loop that equals the orbit loop distance given in the chart.
4. Place the string loop around both pins. Put a pencil inside the loop. Move the pencil so

## Data Table

| Planet/Asteroid | Distance Around Orbit Loop | Distance Between Sun Pin and Second Pin |
|---|---|---|
| Mercury | 13.0 cm | 02.0 cm |
| Venus | 17.6 cm | 00.2 cm |
| Earth | 24.2 cm | 00.4 cm |
| Mars | 39.8 cm | 03.4 cm |
| Asteroid | 140.0 cm | 63.0 cm |

that the string forms a triangle around the pins and the pencil point as shown in the diagram. To draw an orbit, keep the pencil on the paper inside the string loop. Keep the string tight with the pencil and move the pencil around the pins.

### Part Two—Draw Scale Models of Planets

1. With your partner, use a separate sheet of paper to list the information you need to draw scale models of the planets and an asteroid and place them in their proper orbits.
2. Write a brief procedure for drawing the planets.
3. After you have completed your procedure, share your ideas with the class to see if they think your plan will work.

4. Make any needed corrections to your procedure then complete your drawing.

### Part Three—Calculate Eccentricity or How Oval Your Orbit Is

1. After you have completed your drawing, use the orbit models to calculate the eccentricity, or "ovalness," of each planet's orbit.
2. Measure the distance between the foci (pins).
3. Measure the length of the major axis. The major axis is a line that connects the foci then intersects both sides of an orbit.
4. The formula for eccentricity is $(d_f)/(l_a)$ where $(d_f)$ is distance between foci and $(l_a)$ is length of the major axis.
5. Make a data table that shows the values you used and the eccentricity for each orbit on your drawing.

6. After you have completed your work, your teacher will show you the correct eccentricities for the planets.

### Conclusion

Study the orbits you have drawn and add any details or graphics to make it eye-catching. Be careful not to distort the scientific accuracy of the project. You want the public to realize that a collision with an asteroid is definitely going to happen. Write a brief memo to your Graphic Arts Department giving them a summary of the student directions, and be sure to comment on the following topics:

- Is the activity appropriate for middle school students?
- Is the final product something that would make a suitable logo for Asteroid Awareness Education Commission materials?

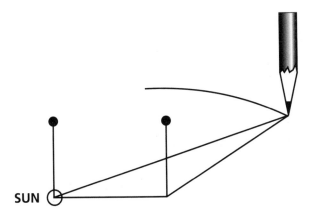

SUN

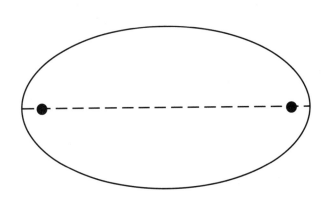

# Things Are Looking Up

When worlds collide, you do not want to be in the way. NASA-sponsored studies of impacts on Earth by comets and asteroids show such an impact takes place over land about once per millennium. Is there an asteroid out there with Earth's name on it? We do not know. If an asteroid with a diameter in the 1-kilometer to 3-kilometer range smashed into Earth, it could cause a global environmental catastrophe.

Being prudent suggests that planet Earth should take the impact hazard as real. Over long time spans, impact catastrophes are inevitable. In short, humans could be annihilated and become the Space Age equivalent of dinosaurs.

As a first step toward planetary protection, a comprehensive search program is likely to be undertaken. One proposed program is Spaceguard Survey. Specially constructed telescopes located around the planet would survey all asteroids that pose the greatest danger to Earth. This equipment would detect an object years before it approached. In the event that enough warning is given to deal with an Earth-approaching asteroid, what could we do?

Such a doomsday rock is not likely to show up at our planetary door.step any time soon. However, a coordinated asteroid avoidance plan would seem wise as Earth's community of nations moves toward the twenty-first century. We are better safe than sorry.

### IN THE NEWS

## 'If it hit you it would squash you'

A 2,000 pound chunk of a Chinese spy satellite is expected to crash to Earth today, probably splashing down in the Pacific Ocean. The precise landing spot won't be known until just a few hours before the expected 1:30 p.m. ET impact.

Out-of-control satellites are like "skipping stones across a pond," says Maj. Nelson McCouch of the U.S. Space Command. "It may veer right, it may veer left. You can't say where it's going to go."

Even if the satellite does hit land, experts say, the risk will be minimal. "If it hit you it would squash you," says John Pike of the Federation of American Scientists. "But the world is big and the satellite is small."— *Jack Williams*

**Written by Steve Marshall.** Contributing: Gary Fields and Carrie Ferguson

*USA TODAY, OCTOBER 28, 1993*

### STUDENT VOICES

I've always loved the sky and stars. It was around August 9 or 10 when I saw my first falling star. At first it took me a second to realize what it was. I was overjoyed and so excited. Then a few days later, the Perseid Meteor shower happened. I heard about it from a friend and I wondered if I would really see anything. I went outside around 8:00 P.M. I was amazed. I had only been outside for ten minutes when it started raining stars. I watched for a good two hours. I saw ones that fell just a little and ones that seemed to fall forever. I'll never forget it and can't wait until I see the next one.

ANNIE FAVOUR
PRESCOTT, ARIZONA

# Rings Around Saturn

Among the planets, Saturn is probably the most beautiful with its spectacularly colorful rings. The outer gaseous planets all have rings, but Saturn's are the most spectacular.

During the 1990s, our perspective will change as we view Saturn's rings edge-on. Normally visible from Earth with a simple telescope, the rings appeared to grow thinner and by 1995 had withdrawn from view, leaving only a pale yellow line. Gradually, the rings will "grow" back as Saturn's tilt appears to change as viewed from Earth. By 2002 the rings will return to center stage once again. This process of "waxing and waning" covers a span of 30 years and is the result of our changing view of the planet.

In addition to its rings, Saturn also has many satellites. Of special interest to scientists is Titan, one of Saturn's largest moons. It carries chemical and atmospheric characteristics similar to those on Earth before life emerged.

Saturn is almost the size of Jupiter. Both have fierce storms, low temperatures, and three-layered cloud belts. Hydrogen and helium are dominant gases on both. The winds of Saturn blow twice as fast as those on Jupiter.

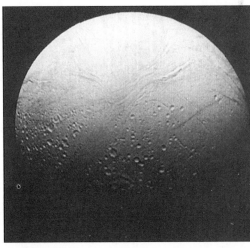

**Voyager 1** *image of Saturn's moon Dione, which has many impact craters*

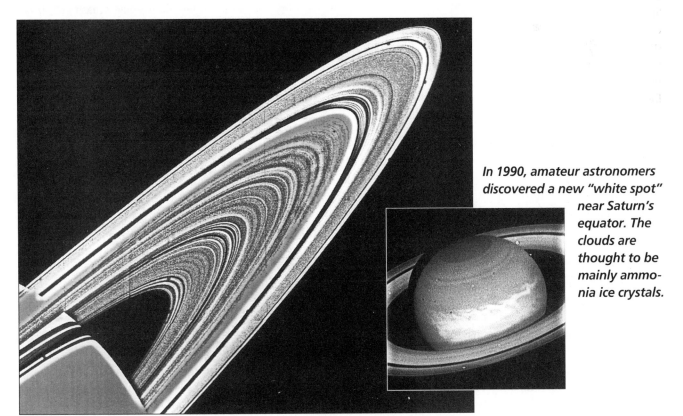

*In 1990, amateur astronomers discovered a new "white spot" near Saturn's equator. The clouds are thought to be mainly ammonia ice crystals.*

*This computer-assembled mosaic shows around 95 individual concentric features in Saturn's rings*

# Amateur Astronomer

**NANCY COX**
**SAN FRANCISCO, CALIFORNIA**

*N*ancy Cox is one of the first ten amateur astronomers who have had the rare opportunity to use NASA's Hubble Space Telescope to conduct original astronomical research. Nancy's observations focused on the Lagoon Nebula. She studied the spectra of hot young stars embedded within the nebula's vast, wispy filaments of gas and dusty streamer.

I have had a natural interest is science all my life. When I was young, I was always catching insects and bees in jars. If a yellow jacket landed on my sandwich, instead of living in terror, I would study it. Also, my mother really encouraged me. She gave me a microscope and took me to the planetarium.

One of my middle school teachers involved us in investigating the science of everyday things—growing sugar crystals from solutions and taking things apart to see how they work. I also collected rocks and minerals, and I knew all the different geologic formations. I was even invited to give a lecture to a class of college students who were studying to be teachers. These types of experiences greatly increased my interest in science.

In the eighth grade I participated in our regional science fair and won an award. The important thing for me was discovering the scientific method on my own—being able to design a controlled experiment. That experience encouraged my interest in

science and how you go about investigating a problem.

I remember enjoying chemistry very much in high school. At that time, they were first discovering DNA (the building blocks of life) and the double helix, and I was reading all about it.

**Nancy Cox, left**

Chemist Marie Curie was one of my heroes. To discover a new element was sort of a dream for me. I was also very curious about our insides and how they work as well as diseases and medicines. Eventually my interest in biology led me into a career as a nurse. I worked in hospital intensive care units for years, but now I am a psychiatric nurse.

Over the years, I also developed a strong interest in astronomy. How molecules have formed into living organisms on this specific planet is very local astronomy. You might look at an atom and the electrons that orbit it as a small solar system.

As an amateur astronomer, I am always an observer. I am constantly poking my head out the window day and night, looking for interesting cloud formations, the halo phenomenon around the Sun, or the interesting twilight colors. By night, I check out the constellations, the planets, and the phase of the Moon.

The reality is that we are on a ball that's spinning in space, hung in a galaxy, and we ourselves are made of the very atoms of the universe. So we are

surrounded by science. You could be studying something every moment no matter where you are. There is always something going on that you can observe.

You don't have to go to a fancy laboratory to find science. It's part of everyday life. We're made of it. It's everywhere you look: the physics of something dropping to the ground, the rainbow colors of oil on the street in the rain, vortexes you see when you stir cream into tea or coffee, and the biology of how a flower opens.

Whether pursuing a career in science, or just trying to appreciate it, math is important. Don't be scared of math. Math is a basic tool that helps you understand science and can offer support in proving your theory is valid.

Chemistry and physics can be fascinating classes. Remember that there are science mysteries to be solved, and don't be afraid to ask questions. Some of those basic questions could involve issues that are still puzzling scientists. Keep questioning everything throughout your life. The scientists who are conducting some of the most exciting research are the ones who are asking those fundamental curious questions.

Some high schools offer classes in astronomy, but if yours doesn't, there are a number of options. Most areas have local amateur astronomy clubs that welcome students of all ages. They usually sponsor lectures on astronomy and often have "star parties." Many groups hold weekend workshops, and some even have classes on how to make your own telescope.

When I saw Saturn through a telescope for the first time, it just blew me away. It wasn't just something in a book. You could go out there and actually find it. Even in the city, you can see the brighter constellations, the planets, and the Moon with all its craters.

The Moon is an alien world just sitting out there in our backyard with all this interesting geology—numerous craters, mountain ranges, and lava flows. There are so many interesting features on the Moon that it could keep you busy for a life time.

If I were the astronomer working on your team and developing a plan to inform the public about the impending disaster of an asteroid impact with Earth, I would consider several factors.

Obviously television is one of the best ways to reach people— the daily news programs, public broadcasting, and science documentaries. I would carefully select experts on asteroid impacts who are very good at explaining things to the public.

We could show video footage of asteroid art, like the paintings by Donald Davis (see page 6). Showing photos of all the known meteor craters worldwide could help too.

Well-written feature articles in the daily newspaper quoting experts would likely be effective, as would coverage in popular news magazines. We might also ask local astronomy clubs and planetariums to provide a lecture series of experts speaking on this serious threat.

## DISCOVERY FILE

# Uranus—The Planet with the Dark Secret

Uranus is the seventh planet in distance from the Sun and is the third largest planet behind Jupiter and Saturn. It is the only planet that is now tipped over on its side with its axis pointing toward the Sun. This unusual position is believed to be the result of a collision with a very large object— possibly a huge comet. What changes would occur on Earth if our North Pole always pointed at the Sun?

The attractive blue-green color of Uranus is due to methane in its upper atmosphere. Other gases present include helium and hydrogen.

Uranus has little in the way of distinctive features. However its five largest moons show amazing diversity of geology. Of the 15 moons of Uranus, 10 were discovered when spacecraft *Voyager 2* flew by in 1986.

All four of the gaseous planets have rings, but the rings surrounding Uranus contain some unidentified dark black material. Speculation connects this dark material to an ancient leftover substance from the origin of the solar system.

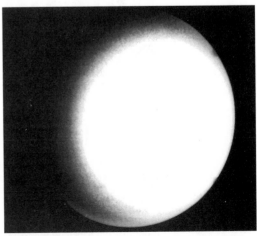

**Voyager 2** *took this picture of Uranus on January 22, 1986.*

# Tuning In on Neptune

Since Neptune is the outermost of the solar system's four giant gas-worlds, it is invisible without a telescope. It was the first planet found by mathematical calculation.

Neptune was named for the Roman god of the sea. It features a Great Dark Spot, fascinating rings, and a small eastward-moving cloud dubbed "scooter" by scientists monitoring the first images sent back by the *Voyager 2* spacecraft in 1989.

Neptune's moon, Triton, is also fascinating. One of its regions looks exactly like the skin of a cantaloupe. Hence the name of the region—the "cantaloupe terrain." Other regions possess equally unusual features, testifying to Triton's remarkable geological history. For example, there are "icy volcanoes"—active geyserlike eruptions spewing invisible nitrogen and dark dust particles into Triton's atmosphere.

Some astronomers offer the capture theory to explain Triton's unusual reverse orbit. They believe it was jerked into that orbit by the gravitational pull of Neptune. Others assert that Triton was originally formed as a natural moon but was later "booted" into its retrograde (backwards) orbit by a celestial impact.

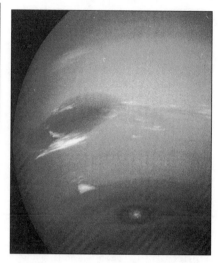

**Neptune, discovered in 1846, is the smallest of the solar system's four gaseous giant planets.**

---

# The sky's the limit for Hubble expert

By Charmagne Helton
USA TODAY

A frustrated Heidi Hammel almost quit her first astronomy class as an undergraduate at Massachusetts Institute of Technology.

You'd never know it now.

Hammel has become a mini-media star as the spokeswoman for the Hubble Space Telescope team. The team, based at Johns Hopkins University in Baltimore, is looking at Comet Shoemaker-Levy 9's collisions with Jupiter.

Hammel is seen on the NASA Select channel, available to some cable subscribers, on other TV programs and quoted in news stories — wherever the celestial phenomenon is the hot topic.

Her commentary is down-to-earth: "I think Jupiter's going to hang in there," she said Monday. "We're seeing these black eyes, big splotches and bruises and I almost feel sorry for Jupiter."

A professor at her alma mater, Hammel has an undergraduate degree in planetary science and a Ph.D. in physics and astronomy.

But her students say she isn't a nerd. She's a Deadhead. "She's a fun person. I don't think she's a nerd," says graduate student Cathy Olkin. "She likes the Grateful Dead. Most nerds wouldn't be considered Grateful Dead fans."

"She's very sharp," says Richard Binzel, MIT associate professor of planetary science. "Heidi can communicate at the most technical level with fellow scientists and then turn around and thoughtfully explain it to the average listener."

Yet Hammel almost didn't make it through her first astronomy class because she had trouble spotting a required celestial phenomenon, says James Elliot, her professor at the time.

When Hammel came to drop the class, Elliot volunteered to help her look at planets: The sky "was clear, we went out and she gathered all her data. So she dropped a history class instead," Elliot laughs. "If it had been cloudy that night, she might not be where she is today."

USA TODAY, JULY 20, 1994

# Pluto and Charon—The Dynamic Duo

The faintest and usually the most distant of the planets are named after Greek and Roman mythological beings. Pluto was king of the underworld and Charon ferried the dead to Hades.

Unlike the other outer planets, Pluto is solid, not gaseous. Pluto's presence was predicted by mathematics and discovered on photographs by Clyde Tombaugh in 1930.

The duo, Pluto and Charon, loop across the orbit of Neptune for a 20-year visit every 248 years. Although they are the smallest residents in our planetary system, they travel the largest orbit around the Sun.

They will be nearest to the Sun at the turn of the century. Scientists will be able to study the frigid, rocky ball and its icy moon at their closest and warmest.

Pluto and Charon share a common gravitational center. They intrigue scientists because the materials they are made of differ. Eager to launch a spacecraft to the double planets by the year 2000, researchers seek data to compare the terrain and atmosphere of Pluto with that of Charon. The spacecraft needs to arrive before Pluto's atmospheric gases freeze and fall to the surface where they and the surface would be less available for study.

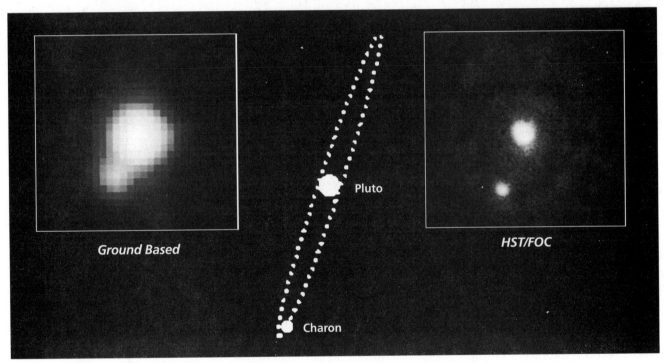

Ground Based

Pluto

Charon

HST/FOC

*NASA's Hubble Space Telescope has obtained the clearest pictures ever of Pluto.*

# Technology Education: Asteroid Smasher

## Purpose

To construct a model "rocket" capable of hitting a 1-foot diameter circular target at a distance of at least 30 feet.

## Materials

**For each student:**
- Wooden pencil
- Pencil cap eraser
- Piece of wire
- Cardboard or poster board (small pieces)

**For the class:**
- Coping saws or mat knives
- Scotch tape or masking tape
- Flat files
- Pliers
- Rubber band(s)

## Procedure

Background: Earth is in danger of being hit by an asteroid. As a rocket scientist, you know that a rocket armed with a bomb could be used to destroy or divert the asteroid. However, the president and Congress are skeptical. You have been asked to build an inexpensive model of such a rocket and demonstrate its effectiveness and reliability. Your ultimate objective is to intercept the asteroid before it impacts Earth, but your immediate objective is to convince the president and Congress that they should fund the project.

Building the model is the easy part. The hard part is making sure it can reliably hit a target. Such variables as the speed of the rocket, the angle of launch, the distance from the target, and the speed of the target need to be tested. You know that for each test only one variable may be tested, and all other variables must be kept constant.

Gather all the information you can. You will only get three chances to destroy an approaching asteroid model. If you fail, funding will be lost and your company will lose a large government contract. But will the people of the world live to regret it? Probably not. Here is how to construct the rocket:

1. About 2.5 centimeters from the eraser end of the pencil, cut or file a small notch, then wrap a short piece of wire around the pencil. The notch will assure that the wire does not slide up and down. Use pliers to twist the wire tightly so that it "bites" into the wood a bit. Next, bend the twisted ends into a hook as shown in the diagram.
2. Use a coping saw or mat knife to cut another notch in the other end of the pencil as shown in the diagram.
3. Cut out small paper rocket fins and tape them to the pencil just above the second notch.
4. Place an eraser cap over the upper end of the rocket. This blunts the nose to make the rocket safer if it hits something. The rocket is now complete.

5. Launch your rocket using the launch pad your teacher will provide.

## Points of Emphasis

1. The rocket's trajectory might be influenced by the

Notch #1

Notch #2

angle of launch and the distance from the asteroid. Can you think of any other factors that might enter into your launch?

2. The fin size may have an effect on your rocket's path.

3. Try launching your rocket with different size rubber bands. What happens?

4. Either individually or in groups of three, come up with an evaluation system that included points for accuracy, construction, and data collection.

5. Produce a data table where the facts about each rocket launch can be recorded. Record such things as the amount of force (number of rubber bands), the angle of launch, distance to the asteroid and the number of hits, near misses, and far misses.

## Conclusion

You have launched your model asteroid smasher. Is Earth saved or doomed? Using the data you collected, explain the success or failure of your rocket.

Note: This activity is adapted from a NASA classroom activity.

# Math: Asteroids and Acceleration

## Purpose

To determine the acceleration of a free-falling body near Earth and to calculate the time it will take a falling object to reach Earth's surface.

## Materials

**Per pair of students:**
- At least 2 meter sticks
- 3 sample asteroids (marbles or balls)
- Ring stand and clamps
- Balance
- Stopwatch
- Sand in a container

**For the class:**
- Balances to find masses of object

## Procedure

Background: You and a partner have been asked to estimate the time of arrival of an asteroid that is now 150,000 kilometers away and approaching Earth on a collision course. You and your partner have decided to conduct an experiment to determine the acceleration of free-falling objects. You plan to use that acceleration to estimate the time of arrival of the asteroid. Be careful, the future of your home town may be at risk!

1. Find acceleration due to gravity of an asteroid near Earth's surface by applying Newton's formula for acceleration (Acceleration = $2d/t^2$). The variable $d$ represents the distance that the asteroid is from Earth. The variable $t$ represents the time (in seconds) it will take for the asteroid to strike Earth.

2. In your experiment, objects of varying masses should be dropped from different heights into a container filled with sand. The time it takes for the object to strike the sand will be recorded, and this information will be used to complete the table.

3. Using this information, you and your partner will determine approximate acceleration due to gravity of a free-falling object. (Drop the same three objects from

### Time Table

| Distance (km) | Acceleration (km/sec²) | Time (minutes) |
|---|---|---|
| 150,000 | 0.0001 | 912.0 |
| 150,000 | 0.001 | 288.0 |
| 150,000 | 0.01 | 91.0 |
| 150,000 | 0.10 | 28.0 |
| 150,000 | 1.00 | 9.0 |
| 150,000 | 10.00 | 2.8 |
| 150,000 | 100.00 | 0.9 |

the given heights.)
4. Compare your results with the other teams.
5. Since the asteroid we are concerned about is 150,000 kilometers from the Earth, the acceleration must be converted from cm/sec² to km/sec². Examples:
789 cm/sec² = .00789 km/sec²
1542 cm/sec² = .01542 km/sec²

Knowing that acceleration = $2d/t^2$, by simple algebra we can show that $t$ = the square root of $2d$/acceleration. The table below uses this formula to determine the time it will take an asteroid that is 150,000 kilometers away, *but with no velocity of its own*, to strike Earth. Using the approximate acceleration that you have determined, find how

much time (in minutes) you have before the asteroid will strike your town.

After presenting your findings to a committee, a brilliant physicist found some major discrepancies in your results. What factor should you have considered for your time estimate to be accurate?

## Acceleration Table

| Mass (grams) | Distance (d) (centimeters) | 2d | Time (t) (seconds) | $t^2$ | Acceleration ($2d/t^2$) |
|---|---|---|---|---|---|
| | 80 | 160 | | | |
| | 80 | 160 | | | |
| | 80 | 160 | | | |
| | 100 | 200 | | | |
| | 100 | 200 | | | |
| | 100 | 200 | | | |
| | 150 | 300 | | | |
| | 150 | 300 | | | |
| | 150 | 300 | | | |
| | 200 | 400 | | | |
| | 200 | 400 | | | |
| | 200 | 400 | | | |
| | 250 | 500 | | | |
| | 250 | 500 | | | |
| | 250 | 500 | | | |

# Social Studies: Known Impact Craters Around the World

## Purpose
To use latitude and longitude to locate impact craters on Earth.

## Materials
- Graph paper
- Asteroid impact map (below)
- Asteroid impact data (page 33)
- Atlas

## Procedure
Background: You and your group have been given the task of selecting a site for the world headquarters of the United Nations' Asteroid Impact Response Team (AIRT). Locating sites of known impact craters worldwide is your first step.

1. Use the Asteroid Impact Map below to construct a bar graph showing approximately how many of the 130 known impact craters are located on each of the continents of the world.
2. Your teacher will give you a list of longitude and latitude coordinates. Determine which of these coordinates are the locations of crater impacts.
3. Your teacher will give you the coordinates of five potential sites for the Asteroid Impact Response Team headquarters. Locate and label each of the sites on the Asteroid Impact Map.

4. Once all five potential headquarter sites have been located and marked, your teacher will assign you one of those sites. Your job is to work with your group to promote that city as the best location for the headquarters of AIRT. Write a presentation to convince others in your class to vote for your city. Also, write a letter to the secretary general of the United Nations stating the location your team recommends. Be sure to use the location of actual impact craters to support your selection.

## Asteroid Impact Map

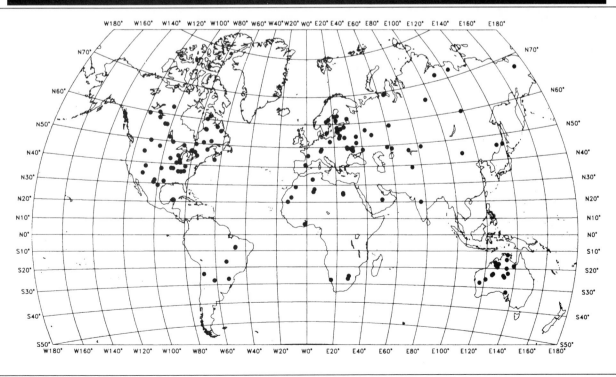

# Asteroid!

## Directions

A worldwide advertising campaign has sparked widespread interest in the disaster about to befall Earth. A large asteroid is on a collision course with Earth. It is due to hit in two years. People all over the planet are arguing about what to do. Opinions vary greatly, but all agree that something must be done. The General Assembly of the United Nations has authorized a worldwide vote to settle the issue.

Get together with four to five neighbors and brainstorm a list of ways we could cope with the coming disaster. You do not have to agree with all opinions presented. Share your group's ideas with the class. Listen carefully to options presented by other groups.

Select the option you like best.

State your choice as a title on a sheet of notebook paper. Explain your choice by listing its advantages and its disadvantages.

Now get together with others who share your choice. Discuss your list of advantages and disadvantages. Modify your list as you hear new ideas with which you agree.

Get together with someone who selected a different course of action than yours. Try to sell your idea to this person, but listen carefully to the points he or she makes. Do this a second time with someone else who has yet another opinion.

Before you vote, think about other viewpoints you have heard. Did one of the opposing viewpoints make more sense to you? Did you change your opinion?

Now you are ready to cast your vote for worldwide action.

Your English teacher may ask you to write about your decision in the form of a *position paper*. Keep all your notes because they will help you with that assignment.

# English: Writing to Persuade

## Purpose

To write a paper defending your position on coping with a coming asteroid impact.

## Materials

- Peer-Response Form (page 55)
- Proofreading Guidesheet (page 56)

## Procedure

Complete the writing activity below. Read the prompt carefully. You may refer to all your previous work in this unit.

## Prompt

You have concluded your investigation of problems related to the impending asteroid disaster. You must now select the best plan for coping with the coming impact.

Write a position paper in which you select and defend a plan for dealing with the asteroid.

Before you begin writing, compare your plan with the plans of others. Does your plan offer the best solution to the problem? What are the comparative advantages of your plan? What evidence can you present to defend your position? What will it take to implement your solution? How much do you think it will it cost? How much time will it take? Who will pay for it? What are the long-term benefits? Are there any disadvantages you can foresee? How can you effectively persuade people and countries to agree with you? Now, write a position paper in which you select, explain, and defend your plan for coping with the coming asteroid's impact on our planet.

## Checklist

1. Have you clearly explained your plan?
2. Have you included all the details needed to gain acceptance for your position?
3. Have you appropriately written to your intended audience, the senators, representatives, and other government leaders who must make the final decision?
4. Have you used evidence and logic to persuade?
5. Have you followed the correct essay format?
6. Have you proofread and edited your paper?

# Peer-Response Form

**Directions**

1. Ask your partners to listen carefully as you read your rough draft aloud.

2. Ask your partners to help you improve your writing by telling you their answers to the questions below.

3. Jot down notes about what your partners say:

   a. What did you like best about my rough draft?

   b. What did you have the hardest time understanding about my rough draft?

   c. What can you suggest that I do to improve my rough draft?

4. Exchange rough drafts with a partner. In pencil, place a check mark near any mechanical, spelling, or grammatical constructions about which you are uncertain. Return the papers and check your own. Ask your partner for clarification if you do not understand or agree with the comments on your paper. Jot down notes you want to remember when writing your revision.

# Proofreading Guidesheet

1. Have you identified the assigned purpose of the writing assignment and have you accomplished this purpose?

2. Have you written on the assigned topic?

3. Have you identified the assigned form your writing should take and have you written accordingly?

4. Have you addressed the assigned audience in your writing?

5. Have you used sentences of different lengths and types to make your writing effective?

6. Have you chosen language carefully so the reader understands what you mean?

7. Have you done the following to make your writing clear for someone else to read:

   - used appropriate capitalization?
   - kept pronouns clear?
   - kept verb tense consistent?
   - made sure all words are spelled correctly?
   - used correct punctuation?
   - used complete sentences?
   - made all subjects and verbs agree?
   - organized your ideas into logical paragraphs?

# BIBLIOGRAPHY

Adams, Peter. *Moons, Mars and Meteorites.* United Kingdom: Her Majesty's Stationary Office for the British Geological Society, 1977.

Asimov, Isaac. *The Asteroids.* New York: Dell Publishing, 1988.

Asimov, Isaac. *Did the Comets Kill the Dinosaurs?* New York: Dell Publishing, 1988.

Arduini, Paolo, and Giorgio Teruzzi. *Simon & Schuster's Guide to Fossils.* New York: Simon and Schuster, Inc., 1986.

Bates, Robyn, and Cheryl Somon. *The Dinosaurs and the Dark Stars.* New York: Macmillan Publishing Company, 1985.

Carlisle, Madelyn. *Let's Investigate Magical, Mysterious Meteorites.* New York: Barrons Educational Series Inc., 1992.

Case, Gerald. *A Pictoral Guide to Fossils.* New York: Van Nostrand Reinhold, 1982.

Clarkson, E. N. K. *Inverterbrate Palaeontology and Evolution.* Second Edition. London: Harper-Collins Academic, 1986.

Dott, Robert, and Roger Batten. *Evolution of the Earth.* Fourth Edition. New York: McGraw Hill Inc., 1988.

Erikson, Jon. *Target Earth! Asteroid Collisions Past and Future.* Blue Ridge Summit, Penn.: TAB Books, 1991.

Kross, John. "Hitting Home: What Happens When Asteroids Out There End Up Down Here?" *Ad Astra,* November/December (1992), pp. 30–32.

Lampton, Christopher. *Mass Extinctions: One Theory of Why the Dinosaurs Vanished.* New York: Franklin Watts, 1982.

Lauber, Patricia. *Meteors and Meteorites—Voyagers from Space.* New York: Thomas Y. Crowell, 1989.

*NASA Magazine,* Summer 1993. Superintendent of Documents, U.S. Government Printing Office, Washington D.C., 20402.

Stanley, Steven. *Earth and Life Through Time.*, Second Edition. New York: Freeman and Company, 1987.

Tufty, Barbara. *1001 Questions Answered About Earthquakes, Avalanches, Floods and Other Natural Disasters.* New York: Dover Publications Inc., 1969.

### General

Follow all instructions. Never perform activities without the approval and supervision of your teacher. Do not engage in horseplay. Never eat or drink in the laboratory. Keep work areas clean and uncluttered.

### Dress Code

Wear safety goggles whenever you work with chemicals, glassware, heat sources such as burners, or any substance that might get into your eyes. If you wear contact lenses, notify your teacher.

Wear a lab apron or coat whenever you work with corrosive chemicals or substances that can stain. Wear disposable plastic gloves when working with organisms and harmful chemicals. Tie back long hair. Remove or tie back any article of clothing or jewelry that can hang down and touch chemicals, flames, or equipment. Roll up long sleeves. Never wear open shoes or sandals.

### First Aid

Report all accidents, injuries, or fires to your teacher, no matter how minor. Be aware of the location of the first-aid kit, emergency equipment such as the fire extinguisher and fire blanket, and the nearest telephone. Know whom to contact in an emergency.

### Heating and Fire Safety

Keep all combustible materials away from flames. When heating a substance in a test tube, make sure that the mouth of the tube is not pointed at you or anyone else. Never heat a liquid in a closed container. Use an oven mitt to pick up a container that has been heated.

### Using Chemicals Safely

Never put your face near the mouth of a container that holds chemicals. Never touch, taste, or smell a chemical unless your teacher tells you to.

Use only those chemicals needed in the activity. Keep all containers closed when chemicals are not being used. Pour all chemicals over the sink or a container, not over your work surface. Dispose of excess chemicals as instructed by your teacher.

Be extra careful when working with acids or bases. When mixing an acid and water, always pour the water into the container first and then add the acid to the water. Never pour water into an acid. Wash chemical spills and splashes immediately with plenty of water.

### Using Glassware Safely

If glassware is broken or chipped, notify your teacher immediately. Never handle broken or chipped glass with your bare hands.

Never force glass tubing or thermometers into a rubber stopper or rubber tubing. Have your teacher insert the glass tubing or thermometer if required for an activity.

### Using Sharp Instruments

Handle sharp instruments with extreme care. Never cut material toward you; cut away from you.

### Animal and Plant Safety

Never perform experiments that cause pain, discomfort, or harm to animals. Only handle animals if absolutely necessary. If you know that you are allergic to certain plants, molds, or animals, tell your teacher before doing an activity in which these are used. Wash your hands thoroughly after any activity involving animals, plants, plant parts, or soil.

During field work, wear long pants, long sleeves, socks, and closed shoes. Avoid poisonous plants and fungi as well as plants with thorns.

### End-of-Experiment Rules

Unplug all electrical equipment. Clean up your work area. Dispose of waste materials as instructed by your teacher. Wash your hands after every experiment.